SPEED SEWING

SPEED SEWING:

103 Sewing Machine Shortcuts

Janice S. Saunders

 VAN NOSTRAND REINHOLD COMPANY
New York Cincinnati Toronto London Melbourne

To Mom

Printed in the United States of America
Designed by Loudan Enterprises

Published by Van Nostrand Reinhold Company Inc.
135 West 50th Street, New York, NY 10020

Fleet Publishers
1410 Birchmount Road
Scarborough, Ontario M1P 2E7, Canada

Van Nostrand Reinhold Australia Pty. Ltd.
480 Latrobe Street
Melbourne, Victoria 3000, Australia

Van Nostrand Reinhold Company Limited
Molly Millars Lane
Wokingham, Berkshire, RG11 2PY England

Library of Congress Cataloging in Publication Data

Saunders, Janice.
  Speed Sewing
  Includes index.
    1. Machine sewing. 2. Needlework. I. Title.
TT713.S25   646.4   80-19523
ISBN 0-442-22488-5

Illustrations by Alan Clever
Photographs by Nicholas Yadlovsky
Design assistance—Elna Sewing Machines

CONTENTS

INTRODUCTION

In traveling from Hawaii to Switzerland and parts in between, I have talked to thousands of women about sewing. What I have heard more than anything else is "I love to sew, but I just don't have the time."

This collection of professional shortcuts will cut sewing time in half, save you money, and help you turn those homemade projects into handmade originals.

I was a home economist fresh out of college when I started promoting sewing throughout the United States. My first job assignment was to cover what has become the contents of this book in a two-hour seminar. I naively assumed that everyone I talked to absorbed all this information with the help of a few illegible notes scrawled on the backs of checkbooks, gum wrappers, and envelopes. Needless to say, one question kept haunting me: Is any of this information written down anywhere?

Alas, it was not. But now, here it is.

With the advent of synthetic fibers, fabrics, and advanced sewing machine technology, the craft of sewing has become a sophisticated art form. Many sewing techniques learned years ago in 4-H and high school home economics classes are no longer useful with modern fabrics and sewing machines. Techniques that were once done only by hand, such as basting, blind-hemming, etc., can now be smoothly executed on a sewing machine. If you know how to sew but are unaware of how to make use of your machine, then you are wasting time and probably not obtaining the professional results you paid dearly for when you bought that sewing machine.

This book is designed to build self-confidence in anyone who wants to renew their interest in sewing. It is also for experts who love to sew and are always trying to put something special into their handmade masterpieces. Finally, it is for all who want to get their money's worth from their sewing machines but never have time to sew.

HOW TO USE THIS BOOK

When baking a pie, you turn to the cookbook section entitled "Pies and Pastry," combine the ingredients, and bake. *Speed Sewing* is used precisely that way, but with a slight twist. Instructions and illustrations for making everything from T-shirts to sweaters are provided, complete with machine settings that apply to any make or model.

In Chapter 1, Sewing Machine History, you will learn that although Isaac Singer claimed he "taught the world to sew," he did not invent the sewing machine. In Chapter 2, three basic sewing machine classifications are explained and coded. From there on, you will learn how to master all kinds of machine shortcuts for almost every type of sewing.

Chapters 3 and 4 discuss important fabric and pattern preparation plus shortcut, machine marking, and basting techniques. This enables you to expedite the necessary, but less interesting, parts of sewing and quickly proceed to the more creative aspects of the craft.

If you lack the confidence or know-how to successfully attach T-shirt ribbing, or cannot get the hang of machine blind hemming, Chapter 5 provides you with the information to achieve the most professional results once the techniques in this chapter are mastered. For example, a nightgown can be cut out at 7:00 P.M., and you will be wearing it by the 11 o'clock news.

Have you ever avoided a pattern because it called for buttonholes? If so, Chapter 6 will teach you easy ways to make both machine and bound buttonholes. In Chapter 7, you will learn how to tastefully update many of your own and your family's wardrobe favorites. Chapter 8 introduces specialty stitching techniques, from the basics of machine appliqué and embroidery to twin-needle work and other machine crafting techniques.

Finally, to keep your machine in tip-top operating order, Chapter 9 highlights machine maintenance and suggests checking possible problem areas before taking your machine in for service.

I have tried to share my trade secrets with you. All but a few of you may read this information and say, "I'll start using some of that stuff next week...next month...or sometime next year." But if you make the excuse that you don't have the time, it is your fault. Please use this book as a handbook kept next to your machine, as a confidence-builder, as an idea book. Use it to make your sewing productive, professional, and fun. Above all, keep on sewing. Let's start making your sewing time count.

Chapter 1

SEWING MACHINE HISTORY

It was not until the last thirty years that tailors, dressmakers, and home sewers have had the luxury of constructing clothing with workable sewing machines. Only within the last thirty years has the sewing machine evolved from a simple mechanical device to join two pieces of fabric together, to a sophisticated piece of machinery that can do almost anything required to produce as elegant or simple a wardrobe as needed.

As early as 1790, Thomas Saint of England experimented with his invention that made a straight stitch with a single thread, a forked needle, and an awl that preceded the needle to poke the hole in the fabric. Although we do not credit the Englishman for the invention of the sewing machine as we know it today, he started other inventors thinking about a machine for sewing clothing.

In 1830, a French tailor named Barthelemy Thimonnier invented the first chain-stitch machine to enjoy any degree of success. The needle penetrated the fabric once, then the thread was pulled around a looper under the needle and held there until the second stitch was made. As one loop dropped into the other, a chain stitch was formed. Two pieces of cloth could successfully be joined as the fabric was moved *by hand* under the needle (figure 1-1). The flaw in this system was its lack of a proper feeding mechanism.

Between 1832 and 1834, the

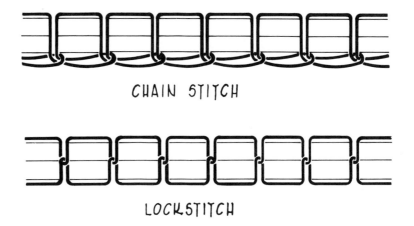

CHAIN STITCH

LOCKSTITCH

Figure 1-1 Chain stitch and lockstitch.

first lockstitch machine was invented by Walter Hunt, an American from New York. A lockstitch is made with the use of two threads; one is used through a grooved needle, the other is on a shuttle or *bobbin* (figure 1-1). The fabric was fed vertically on a movable frame and had to be constantly reset after a short run of stitches.

A newcomer named Elias Howe registered his third sewing machine with the U.S. Patent Office in 1845, with the British Patent Office in 1846, and has been officially credited with the invention of the sewing machine. With the wide-scale introduction of the Howe machine, sewing machines became more suitable for both consumer and industrial use in making ready-to-wear apparel.

It was not until 1851, when Isaac Singer produced a simpler lockstitch mechanism with a presser foot, straight needle, and a horizontal bed that machine sewing became even more practical. After refining Singer's system, Allen B. Wilson discovered an even more effective way to make a lockstitch by adding his four-motion feed system, what today is commonly called the *feed dog* (figure 1-2).

By the second half of the nineteenth century, the Wheeler and Wilson sewing machine incorporated most elements found in modern home sewing machines. Although industrial sewing machines have been powered by electricity since 1889, domestic machines had to wait until electricity was available for household consumption. Until that time, machines were operated by hand crank or foot treadle.

By the end of the Civil War, Thomas White introduced the New England sewing machine that improved the lockstitch by means of a take-up lever and added the first numbered upper-thread tension-control system. White also introduced the first sewing machine with a suitcase-type carrying case in 1887, and thus began the era of the portable sewing machine.

Isaac Singer's name has long been associated with home sewing. Besides adding many improvements to the basic machine, his partner, Edward Clark, became the father of another industry.

By the end of the nineteenth century, no household was complete without a sewing machine, even though they were very costly. Edward Clark developed the *hire system* of selling, whereby he extended credit to his customers. This system has had more economic importance in the twentieth century than the development of the sewing machine itself. It is no wonder that sewing with a machine became so

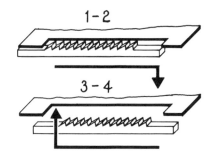

Figure 1-2 Feed movement.

popular; it cut sewing time by 75 percent and was easily affordable, too. By 1900, annual sewing machine production was over twenty-million units, manufactured by over 200 different companies. Only a handful of those companies are still in business today.

Because sewing machines were meant to be used in households around the world, they were made of cast iron and solidly built. Providing that the home sewer kept the machine cleaned, oiled, and changed needles regularly, it would outlive the owner! Treadle machines are still prevalent in many parts of the world today including the United States, and for that reason are not valuable as collectors' items.

As early as 1882, John Kaiser developed the first zigzag machine stitch which opened a new world of sewing possibilities. This innovation, however, only became commonly available on domestic sewing machines with the wide-spread use of synthetic fabrics in the mid-1940s. Although the zigzag stitch was designed to save time, it was not used as much as it could have been for decorative work and mending, which started inventors thinking once again.

During the depression, a young Spaniard named Ramon Cassas watched his mother mend socks and patch knee holes by hand. Her sewing machine sat idle. He thought he could redesign the sewing machine so that most household mending could be done quickly and easily. He changed the shape of the bed of the machine to a free arm, making it easy to sew around circular items such as socks, sleeves, and pants cuffs. He determined the proper diameter for the free arm by measuring women's ankles in train stations all over Europe. By 1939, his innovative free-arm sewing machine was introduced to the home sewing market under the name Elna. The Elna introduced numbered bobbin tension, universal thread tensions, and universal presser foot pressure. By 1952 it was the first machine with a stretch stitch—the featherstitch.

Stretch stitches are made by the forward and reverse motion of the feed dog. The featherstitch was the first stitch of this kind made by a sewing machine and was accomplished by engaging the stitch-width control. The fabric moves back and forth while the needle moves from side to side. When the stitch width is disengaged, the fabric still feeds forward and backward, but the needle no longer swings from side to side. The resulting stitch, called the "straight stretch stitch," is made the same way as the hand backstitch (two stitches forward, one back) and is used the same way—to reinforce stress areas of a garment. The stretch stitch is copied from the hand backstitch and is the basis of all reverse-action stretch and decorative stitches.

This new stitch configuration, used for reinforcing stress seams (pocket, underarm, and crotch seams), opened another door to practical and creative sewing which gave the home sewer faster, more professional results. But the real potential of stretch stitches was not recognized until knit fabrics were available to home sewers during the 1960s. Today most sewing machine manufacturers build stretch stitches into their sewing machines in all price ranges.

No matter what combination of features or stitches are built into your machine, nothing is going to help speed up or professionalize your sewing more than knowing how to properly utilize this equipment.

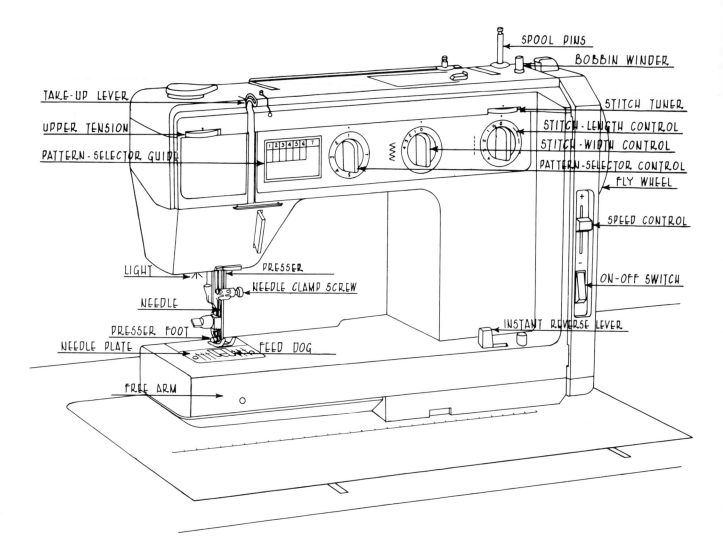

SPOOL PINS

BOBBIN WINDER

TAKE-UP LEVER

STITCH TUNER

UPPER TENSION

STITCH-LENGTH CONTROL

PATTERN-SELECTOR GUIDE

STITCH-WIDTH CONTROL

PATTERN-SELECTOR CONTROL

FLY WHEEL

SPEED CONTROL

LIGHT

PRESSER

ON-OFF SWITCH

NEEDLE CLAMP SCREW

NEEDLE

PRESSER FOOT

NEEDLE PLATE

FEED DOG

INSTANT REVERSE LEVER

FREE ARM

Figure 2-1 Parts of a sewing machine.

Chapter 2

GET ON SPEAKING TERMS WITH YOUR SEWING MACHINE

I cannot tell you how often I have asked home sewers what kind of sewing machine they own. Some cannot tell me the color, brand name, if it zigzags, or its age, but inevitably I am told "it is in perfect condition," "has never been out of the box," or "it is the one that does everything."

The point is, even if your machine slices, dices, chops, and liquifies, the most important thing to know is what stitches it can sew. More specifically, what classification does your machine fit into. There are three basic types of sewing machines. Figure 2-1 identifies parts of the sewing machine common to the three different classifications:

Straight-stitch class
Zigzag class
Reverse-action class

STRAIGHT-STITCH SEWING MACHINE

Straight-stitch sewing machines are generally twenty years old or older and may be powered by foot treadle or electricity. The only stitch possible on this type of sewing machine is the familiar straight stitch used for basting, straight seams, and topstitching in basic garment construction. Other possibilities are limited to the kind of attachments available for your machine, and your skill as the operator.

The straight-stitch sewing machine has one basic control, *the stitch length* (figure 2-2) which regulates the movement of the feed dog. The feed dog advances the fabric under the presser foot.

STITCH LENGTH

STRAIGHT STITCH

Figure 2-2 Straight-stitch sewing machine.

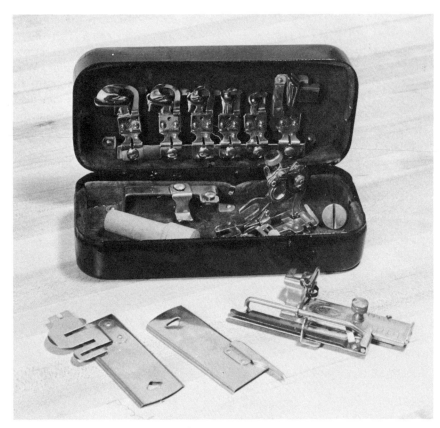

Figure 2-3 Sewing machine attachments.

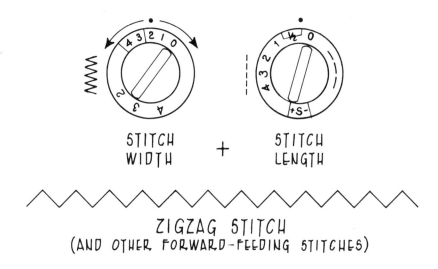

STITCH WIDTH + STITCH LENGTH

ZIGZAG STITCH
(AND OTHER FORWARD-FEEDING STITCHES)

Figure 2-4 Zigzag sewing machine.

The distance the fabric moves each time determines the length of the stitch as the needle moves up and down.

In the 1940s, machines were developed with the ability to sew in reverse, to back tack or lock stitches off at the end of seams, saving time formerly spent in tieing off threads at the ends of seams. Many other accessories or attachments came as standard equipment with straight-stitch machines and were designed to save time. This included the ruffler, buttonholer, binder, rolled-hem foot, and zigzag attachment (figure 2-3). But as fabrics changed from natural wovens to synthetics, blends, and knits of all kinds, home sewers wanted these time-saving features built into their sewing machines.

ZIGZAG SEWING MACHINE

The zigzag sewing machine has a stitch-length control, like the straight-stitch model, plus a *stitch-width* control that automatically moves the needle from side to side, creating different stitch patterns. The most common is the zigzag stitch (figure 2-4).

With the zigzag stitch, buttons can be sewn on by machine, and buttonholes and monograms can be made without special attachments. Seams can be overcast quickly by machine to prevent raveling. The zigzag sewing machine is often confined to the simple zigzag stitch. Other stitches built into zigzag sewing machines may include the following (figure 2-5):

Multiple-zigzag or three-step zigzag stitch: This stitch is used for overcasting raw edges, instant patching and mending, understitching, elastic application, smocking, and twin-needle work. It is better than the zigzag stitch for these jobs because the fabric will not tunnel, or curl under the stitch.

Blind-hem stitch: Used to invisibly hem woven fabrics, the blind-hem stitch saves time-consuming hand hemming. It can also be used to make the shell stitch commonly found on lingerie and T-shirt hems.

Stretch blind-hem stitch: This stitch has a similar function to the blind-hem stitch but is designed for use on knit fabrics.

The extra thread in the stitch allows knit hems sewn with the stretch blind-hem stitch to stretch and give with the garment. When used on a short stitch length, the stretch blind-hem stitch can also be used as a decorative edge finish or topstitch on placemats, napkins, and appliqués.

Interlock or overedge stitch:

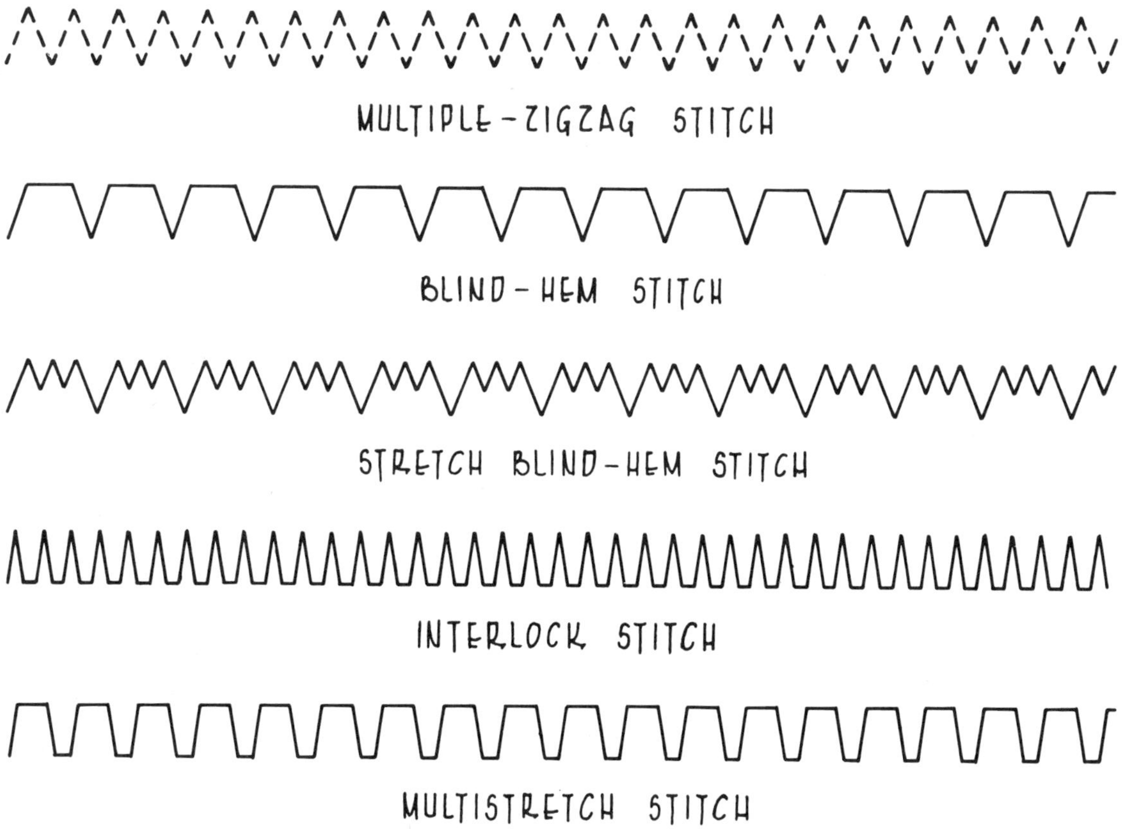

MULTIPLE-ZIGZAG STITCH

BLIND-HEM STITCH

STRETCH BLIND-HEM STITCH

INTERLOCK STITCH

MULTISTRETCH STITCH

Figure 2-5 Utility zigzag stitches.

This stitch, available on newer zigzag models, was developed to seam very lightweight fabrics, such as tricot, Qiana, chiffon, batiste, silk, and organza. The interlock, as it is commonly known, stitches and finishes a narrow seam in one step, eliminating the necessity for French seams on fine fabric.

Multistretch stitch: Designed to stitch and overcast some knit seams in one step, the multistretch stitch is often used for elastic application and smocking, and found on only more recent zigzag models.

Decorative stitches: Used to personalize table linens, gift items, and accent clothing, decorative stitches are sometimes created with special sewing machine accessories and presser feet. Two or more such stitches are often built in on zigzag models (figure 2-6).

TRACERY SCALLOP STITCH

BALL STITCH

DIAMOND STITCH

DOMINO STITCH

CHECKER STITCH

SCALLOP STITCH

Figure 2-6 Decorative zigzag stitches.

REVERSE-ACTION SEWING MACHINE

This type of sewing machine has a stitch-length control and a stitch-width control like the zig-zag sewing machine. It also has a *stitch selector* that engages the machine for a reverse-action stitch. The stitch selector can be a dial, a push-button, or a touch-sensitive panel. What makes this machine different is the ability of the feed dog to move the fabric forward and backward as the needle swings from side to side. This four-way movement is either built in or activated by inserting cassettes, special discs, or cams, each with different stitch patterns (figure 2-7).

Most sewing machines built within the last ten to twelve years have this special stitching capability, allowing you to create many functional and beautiful decorative stitches. The most important feature of reverse-action

machines is their ability to sew stretch stitches, which are used to professionally construct a knit garment.

As more knit and synthetic fabrics became available to home sewers, older model sewing machines could not handle them without skipped stitches or puckered seams. Reverse-action machines are the perfect solution to the problem, especially for knit seams, because the stitches have a *memory*. These stitches will stretch and are strong enough that the thread will not break in the seam with the movement of the garment. Stretch stitches are also used to expedite the construction of woven garments because they can stitch and finish seams in one step. Reverse-action sewing machines offer a wide stitch selection, including some or all of the stitches described as follows (figure 2-8):

Straight-stretch stitch: Designed to reinforce areas of stress

(underarm seams, pocket seams, and crotch seams), the straight-stretch stitch should only be used after fitting the garment, because it is almost impossible to rip out if you make a mistake.

Serging stitch: The serging stitch is made by an industrial sewing machine to expedite the construction of ready-to-wear clothing. The stitch sews and overcasts the seam in one operation. For your point of reference, look inside a ready-to-wear T-shirt or other piece of clothing. In most cases, the seams are "serged" to prevent them from ravelling.

Overlock stitch: This is a serging stitch copied for home use from an industrial stitch used to make ready-to-wear, and is common on reverse-action sewing machines. This stitch can be used to stitch and finish ¼-inch (6 mm.) seams in one operation on woven and knit fabrics, and for sewing elastic on lingerie.

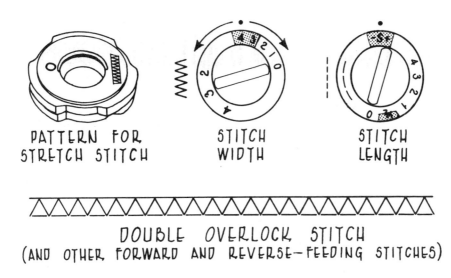

PATTERN FOR STRETCH STITCH

STITCH WIDTH

STITCH LENGTH

DOUBLE OVERLOCK STITCH
(AND OTHER FORWARD AND REVERSE-FEEDING STITCHES)

Figure 2-7 Reverse-action sewing machine.

Double overlock stitch: Besides stitching and finishing a seam in one step, the double overlock stitch is popular as a topstich on T-shirts, jeans, and sportswear. The double overlock stitch is most often used as a seam finish on such woven fabrics as gabardine, corduroy, and denim.

Super-stretch or overlock stitch: The super-stretch stitch, as it is most commonly called, is effective on extremely stretchy fabrics such as sweater-knit and swimsuit fabric. The super-stretch stitch sews and overcasts a ¼-inch (6 mm.) seam in one operation, stretches with the fabric when worn, then enables seams to return to their original shape.

Picot or super-jersey stitch: A French term also describing a hand stitch used to sew lace on the finest French lingerie, the picot stitch is used for sewing fine seams and lace appliqués. It is often considered a problem solver because it is used to seam fine fabrics without puckering.

A reverse-action machine allows you to make special decorative stitches, some of which look like hand embroidery. These stitches can be useful, as well as pretty, for topstitching hems and other time-saving purposes (figure 2-9).

Couching stitch: This stitch is used to stitch over or *couch down* ribbon, soutache braid, or embroidery floss to make a bold, tailored topstitch or trim. The couching stitch may also be used to shell-hem lingerie.

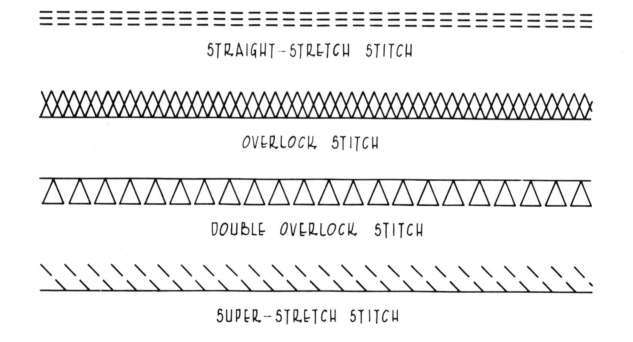

STRAIGHT-STRETCH STITCH

OVERLOCK STITCH

DOUBLE OVERLOCK STITCH

SUPER-STRETCH STITCH

PICOT STITCH

Figure 2-8 Utility reverse-action stitches.

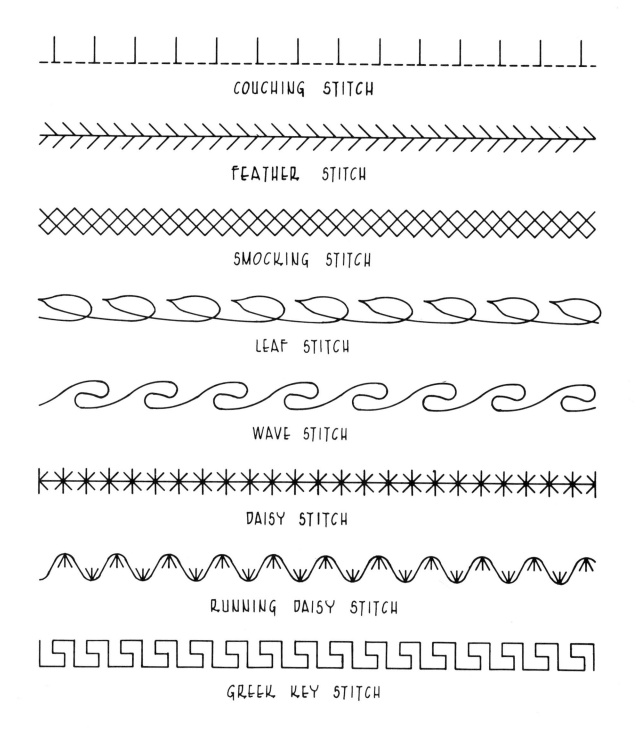

COUCHING STITCH

FEATHER STITCH

SMOCKING STITCH

LEAF STITCH

WAVE STITCH

DAISY STITCH

RUNNING DAISY STITCH

GREEK KEY STITCH

Figure 2-9 Decorative reverse-action stitches.

Featherstitch: Frequently used in machine quilting, the featherstitch is a copy of the popular hand-embroidered featherstitch.

Smocking stitch: This stitch is used when machine smocking needs to resemble hand smocking, but takes a lot less time. The smocking stitch can also be used as a seam finish for wovens that ravel or knit fabrics such as velour or stretch terry cloth.

Leaf stitch: This stitch is an example of the kind of realistic design the reverse-action machine can make, and is used for decorative sewing.

Wave stitch: This stitch is most often used on lingerie hems and to decorate children's clothing.

Daisy stitch: This stitch is commonly used as a hemstitch on lightweight woven fabrics, such as handkerchief linen, which are used to make fingertip towels, dresser scarves, or delicate blouses.

Running daisy: The running daisy stitch can be used to couch over a piece of ribbon, braid, or used in machine smocking.

Greek key: This classic-looking stitch is used as a decorative topstitch, to couch over ribbon, trim, or to finish lingerie hems.

The next time you sit down to sew, introduce yourself to the special stitches available on your sewing machine. Test each one—some are sure to be favorites—then use the stitches as explained in the following chapters for fast professional results. You may even discover some special uses for them on your own that will save you more time when sewing.

PRESSER FEET

Fastened with a screw or snapped on to the presser bar, presser feet hold the fabric in place under the needle. The following are some of the presser feet commonly available for most sewing machines. Although differences in some presser feet are not immediately apparent when looking at them on the sewing machine, all their variations are found by looking at them upside down.

Straight-stitch foot: The straight-stitch foot is generally only found on straight-stitch machines. The needle goes down into a small hole in the needle plate while the fabric is held firmly by the presser foot. On straight-stitch sewing machines, the foot is usually narrow with two toes, one thicker and sometimes longer than the other. The straight-stitch foot and needle plate can be used to sew very fine silk and silklike fabrics.

Zigzag foot: Made of metal and often with a nonstick coating for smooth sewing, the zigzag foot has a wide, oval hole in it to accommodate the zigzag stitch. This hole sometimes causes the needle to push lightweight fabrics through the needle plate when sewing with a straight stitch, and you have to stop and pull the fabric out of the machine. It is for this reason that many zigzag sewing machines are built so the needle can be positioned to the left of center. This is commonly referred to as *left needle position.* With the needle to the left, there is close support around three sides of the needle so the fabric is held firmly between the foot and feed dog while stitching. Some manufacturers offer both a straight-stitch needle plate with a small round hole for straight stitching, and a zigzag needle plate with a wide, oval hole for all other stitch settings.

The zigzag foot can be used to sew fine fabrics when the needle is positioned to the left, and medium to heavy fabrics when the needle is positioned in the center. This way, you will not have to change the needle plate for zigzag sewing.

Embroidery foot: The embroidery foot has a wide channel behind the needle hole enabling embroidery stitches to move smoothly under the foot without flattening them into the fabric. The embroidery foot is recommended for use on medium weight fabrics such as kettle cloth and wool flannel, and is often made of a clear, see-through material for better visibility.

Now turn the zigzag foot over and compare it to the underside of the embroidery foot (figure 2-10). The zigzag foot is flat and firmly supports the fabric around the needle, which reduces the occurrence of skipped stitches and/or puckered seams. The zigzag foot is recommended for use on very fine fabrics such as crepe de chine, and Qiana, and on very heavy fabrics such as denim, leather and leatherlike fabrics, corduroy, and upholstery fabrics.

Buttonhole feet: Buttonhole feet come in various shapes and sizes. The underside of a conventional buttonhole foot has a wide

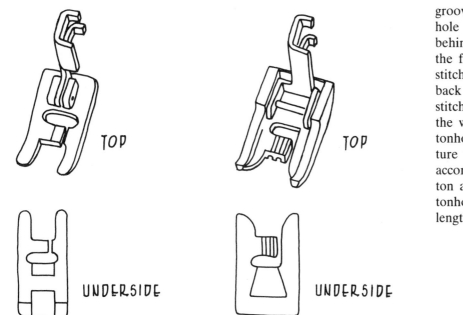

TOP

TOP

UNDERSIDE

UNDERSIDE

groove in front of the needle hole and two smaller channels behind it. The wide groove in the front will not flatten the stitches, while the grooves in the back of the foot move over the stitches already made to guide the work accurately. Some buttonhole feet have a built-in feature that measures the buttonhole according to the size of the button and ensures that each buttonhole will be made the same length (figure 2-11).

Figure 2-10 Zigzag foot (left) and embroidery foot (right).

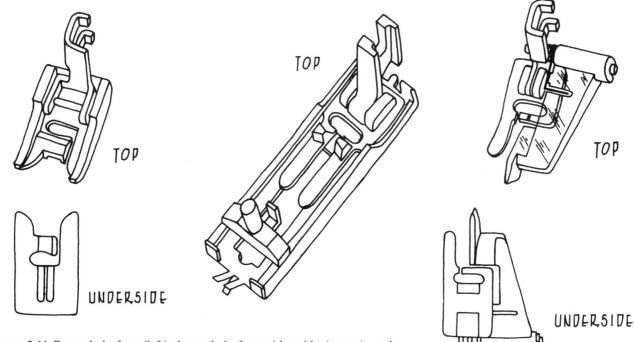

TOP

TOP

TOP

UNDERSIDE

UNDERSIDE

Figure 2-11 Buttonhole foot (left), buttonhole foot with guide (center), and blind-hem foot (right).

SPECIALTY PRESSER FEET

These feet are designed to assist you in specific sewing tasks. Each foot, while it can be used on most fabrics, usually has one specific purpose.

Blind-hem foot: Although this presser foot is not absolutely necessary to sew a blind hem, you will find it is worth having because hems can be sewn much faster and more invisibly. The blind-hem foot (figure 2-11) has a blade or edge that is placed against the fold of the hem to guide the stitching. It may also be used for making accurate pin tucks, stitched creases on slacks, and to topstitch the edge of pleats.

Button-sewing foot: The button-sewing foot makes sewing on buttons much faster and easier. There are two types of button-sewing feet. One has a rubber sleeve on the front, which prevents the button from slipping, and an open toe to facilitate seeing the holes of the button easily. The second type of button-sewing foot is made the same way, but has an adjustable *shank-maker* that can be moved to create a suitable shank length between the button and the garment (figure 2-12).

Gathering foot: The gathering foot (figure 2-12) is used to make ruffles in a fraction of the time it used to take. Lightweight cotton, blends, and batistes are recommended for use with the gathering foot.

Pin-tucking foot: Tucks are delicate touches found on blouses, front yokes, and along sleeves. To make this job more accurate and much easier, the pin-tucking foot (figure 2-12) was developed for use with a twin needle. A twin needle is actually two needles joined into one shank. Check your instruction manual to see if your machine can use a twin needle. *Note:* This foot and the twin needle are only suitable for machines with top and front-loading bobbins.

The pin-tucking foot has many narrow channels under it. After the first tuck is made, the rest are lined up with it and evenly spaced, using the channels in the foot as a guide (figure 2-12). This time-saving technique does not require extra yardage because twin-needle tucks do not take up as much fabric as do traditional pin tucks.

Cording and braiding foot: Have you ever tried sewing on soutache braid or tiny rickrack?

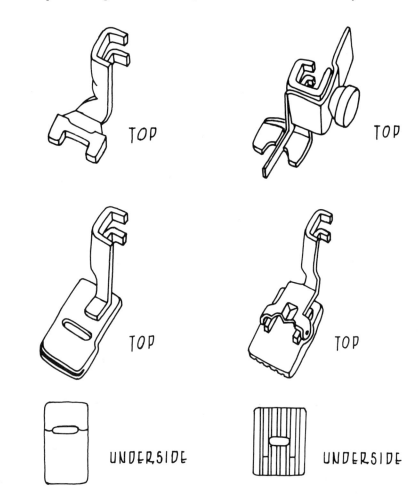

Figure 2-12 Button-sewing foot (above left), gathering foot (below left), button-sewing foot with shank maker (above right), pin-tucking foot (below right).

The cording foot (figure 2-13) can turn that tedious job into a pleasant job. It has a clip or adjustable hole that accommodates up to a ¼-inch (6 mm.) trim (figure 2-13). Once threaded with cord, yarn, or braid, the deep groove under the foot keeps the trim in place. Even when moving the trim to stitch in different directions, the stitches will not *run off* the braid. This foot is a must for anyone who makes uniforms, square-dance clothing, and other costumes.

Fringe foot: At first glance, this foot does not seem to serve a useful purpose, but the fringe foot can save a lot of time spent in marking pattern pieces and serves as a creative tool in decorative sewing.

The fringe foot (figure 2-13) is

built with one or two ¼-inch (6 mm.) vertical blades. As the needle zigzags over the blades, a loopy chenille effect is created. For tailor tacking, a few stitches of fringe are sewn, then cut like a tailor's tack to mark a dart, pleat, or tuck placement. When the stitches are sewn closer together, the foot can be used for various machine embroidery techniques.

Roller foot: The roller foot has diamond-pointed rollers which help feed heavy fabrics. It is particularly helpful when sewing across heavy intersecting seams in denim, fur and furlike fabric, corduroy, and canvas, because the rollers move over uneven seams to prevent seams from moving and shifting (figure 2-14).

Thin-material or walking foot:

The thin-material or walking foot was designed for sewing lightweight fabrics, matching plaids and stripes, and sewing synthetic suedes. It has a bar that rests on the needle-clamp screw; so when the needle is out of the fabric, the teeth of the foot rise up off the fabric with the needle. When the needle is in the fabric, the teeth in the foot hold the fabric in place during stitch formation. This light touch helps prevent puckering and fabric shifting when matching plaids and stripes. If your machine does not have such a foot to fit it, check your instruction manual to see how to loosen the pressure on the presser foot. Many sewers also use this foot to sew stretchy fabrics when sewing a long seam (figure 2-14).

Overcast guide-foot: The overcast guide-foot prevents fabric edges from tunneling, or curling under, when overcasting an edge. The bar across the needle hole keeps the fabric flat, and the wing in the foot makes guiding the fabric easier. This foot is especially valuable when overcasting a lightweight fabric with a zigzag or overlock stitch (figure 2-14).

Zipper foot: The zipper foot has one toe on it that can be moved first to sew one side, then the other side of the zipper (figure 2-15).

Quilting foot and guide: Although quilting has traditionally been done by hand, beautiful quilted effects can be created by machine. The quilting foot is similar to the zipper foot because it has one toe, enabling you to

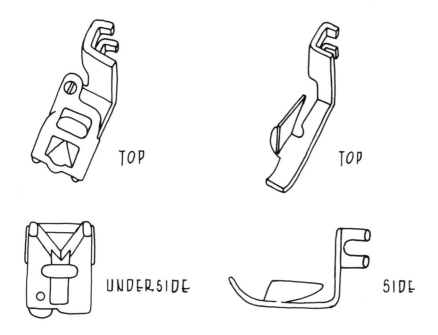

Figure 2-13 Cording and braiding foot (left) and fringe foot (right).

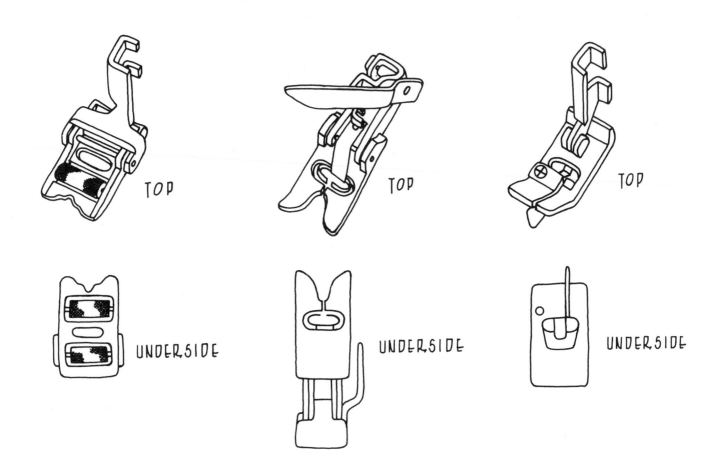

Figure 2-14 Roller foot (left), thin-material or walking foot (center), overcast guide-foot (right).

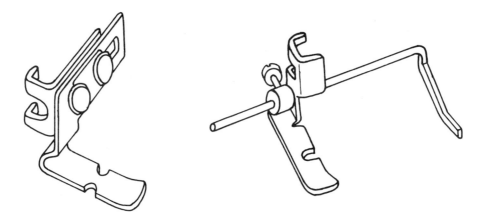

Figure 2-15 Zipper foot (left) and quilting foot with guide.

quilt in hard-to-sew areas close to appliqués and/or blanket binding. The quilting guide slides into an adjustable hole or slot to the right of the foot. It can be moved in and out for quilting even, consecutive rows. Some machines have a second quilting guide that fits on the left side of the foot; so rows of quilting can be sewn up to five inches (12.7cm.) apart.

The quilting foot and guide can also be used for making upholstery piping by moving the guide closer to the foot (figure 2-15).

These special feet can open a whole new world of sewing fun and creativity. Many sewing machines come equipped with some or all of these presser feet and are designed to make your sewing easier and give you more professional results. Many manufacturers are continually creating new feet and accessories. Keep in touch with your local dealer to find out what is new.

PRESSER FOOT PRESSURE

On every sewing machine, the presser foot exerts pressure against the fabric and feed dog. This insures proper stitch formation because the fabric is held firmly in place as the stitch is made. Sometimes, however, very fine or very heavy fabrics may not move well under the foot, requiring a pressure adjustment.

Old straight-stitch models have a screw-type pressure adjustment found on the top of the machine directly above the needle. Newer models may have a button or recessed dial located in the same place which can be adjusted for normal sewing and gradually released for heavy fabrics (figure 2-16). Other, more expensive sewing machines may have a pressure that adjusts automatically to any type, weight, or thickness of fabric.

Sewing Through Bulk

To sew thick or bulky fabrics, place the zigzag or roller foot on your machine. If your machine has a pressure adjustment, you may have to release the pressure slightly to fit the fabric under the presser foot. When approaching a heavy seam, lift the fabric in front of the foot until the uneven seam or thickness is under the toe. Many presser feet are hinged and, as the foot approaches the thickness, the hinge allows the

FULL PRESSURE

PRESSURE RELEASED

Figure 2-16 Pressure.

toe to tip up on the seam. In this case, only the back part of the feed dog is feeding the fabric, which sometimes causes skipped stitches and stitch distortion. After the foot is on the seam, push down on the toe of the foot so it is level with the fabric and feed dog. When you are finished sewing thick fabrics, be sure to return the pressure to the *full* pressure position so other fabrics will not slip under the foot (figure 2-16).

TENSION

Thread tension is one of the most feared parts of the sewing machine, but it does not have to be. There are two areas of thread tension, the upper thread tension located on the top of the machine and usually regulated with a numbered dial, and the lower bobbin tension located on the bobbin case. Some machines have a built-in, top-loading bobbin case with a preset bobbin tension; others have a removable bobbin case. If you have a removable bobbin case, start there with your tension adjustments, then balance the upper tension to the bobbin tension afterward.

To adjust tension on a bobbin case, thread bobbin for normal sewing. Locate the tension screw on the side of the bobbin case, and loosen it by turning it counterclockwise. Tension should be loosened enough to allow bobbin thread to be pulled without any drag on the thread. *Hint:* Do not loosen tension screw so much that the screw pops out.

Now, tighten the tension screw

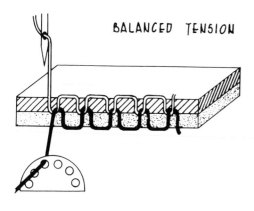

BALANCED TENSION

TOP TENSION TOO TIGHT

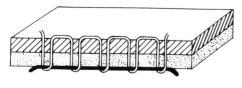

TOP TENSION TOO LOOSE

Figure 2-17 Tension.

by turning it clockwise, a quarter turn at a time. Hold the thread end so the bobbin and bobbin case are up in the air. If the bobbin and bobbin case slip down the thread, you must tighten the tension screw by quarter turns until the thread holds the weight of the bobbin and bobbin case without slipping down the thread. Then tighten the tension screw another quarter turn. *Note:* After you have properly adjusted the bobbin tension, balance the upper thread tension to the lower thread tension by adjusting the upper tension *only* (figure 2-17). If, after adjusting the bobbin, you find it will not keep an even tension, the bobbin case may be worn out. Invest in a new case.

To test the tension on straight-stitch machines, adjust the bobbin tension as described and sew a row of straight stitches (about twelve stitches per inch) on the bias of a doubled piece of woven cotton fabric. Grasp the fabric at both ends of the stitching line and pull. If both the top and the bobbin threads break, the thread tension is balanced. If the top thread only breaks, the upper tension is too tight and

must be loosened to balance with the bobbin tension. If the bobbin thread breaks, the upper tension is too loose and must be tightened until it is balanced with the bobbin tension. After proper adjustment, threads should lock between the two pieces of fabric (figure 2-17).

For zigzag and reverse-action machines, I prefer checking tension by using a long, wide zigzag stitch. Sew a row of zigzag stitches on the bias of a doubled piece of woven cotton fabric. Turn the work over and look at the stitch quality. If the bobbin thread has been pulled to the top of the fabric, loosen the top tension. If the top thread has been pulled to the underside, tighten the upper tension.

Note: Some zigzag and reverse-action sewing machines with built-in bobbin cases have universal top and bobbin tensions that adjust to any fabric. In this case, thread tensions are preset and do not usually require special adjustments by the home sewer. If your machine has a built-in bobbin case with tension problems, see your local sewing machine dealer for help.

Chapter 3

TOOLS OF THE TRADE

There are many factors that determine your sewing success or failure. To be successful, you must have the proper equipment, supplies, and an understanding of fibers and fabrics. Your sewing machine must be clean and oiled and have a new needle that is the right size and type for your project. (See Chapter 9).

Be organized. If you cut your fabric in a place other than your sewing area, have an extra supply of pins, a ruler, a measuring tape, and sharp shears handy. Try organizing your sewing area so supplies are at your fingertips. You will speed up your sewing if you eliminate running all over the place for thread, zippers, elastics, etc. You may want to plan your sewing area like those illustrated (figures 3-1, 3-2).

Organize other sewing tools on a pegboard, or use one of the many sewing organizers on the

Figure 3-1 Sewing room.

Figure 3-2 Sewing room.

FIBER VERSUS FABRIC

market. The one pictured is great for small places. It turns on its base and holds almost anything a home sewer needs near the sewing machine (figure 3-3).

The fiber content of a fabric is responsible for its *wearability,* whether it has to be dry-cleaned or is machine washable, whether it wrinkles or stains. Natural fibers (cotton, silk, wool, linen) and synthetic fibers (polyester, acrylic, nylon, etc.), or a combination of both types of fibers are spun into threads or yarns, then woven or knitted into fabric. The way a fabric is woven or knitted determines the way it should be sewn, the comfort, fit, and what type garment is most appropriate for that fabric. Pattern companies always recommend the best types of fabrics for each design for these reasons.

Woven fabrics are made on looms with lengthwise yarns called the *warp,* and filler, or crosswise, yarns called the *weft* or *woof.* Using computer programs for the fabric design, fiber yarns are woven with one or many shuttles moving in and out of the warp fibers to make a piece of cloth. The long, finished edges parallel with the warp are the *selvage edges.* The yarns can be woven into a textured gabardine, houndstooth or herringbone tweed, or colorful plaid. Because the warp and weft yarns are stable, and only have an ability to stretch on the *bias* (figure 3-4), woven fabrics require extra fitting with seams, gathers, darts, and tucks. Wovens also require a little more attention before final stitching, because raw edges should be overcast or finished in some way to prevent raveling.

Knits, on the other hand, are made from continuous yarns knitted into a series of loops to create the fabric. Single knits, such as nylon tricot, are made with a single set of needles, and the edges of this fabric roll to the right side when the goods are stretched on the cross grain. Some single knits have noticeable courses, called *ribs,* that run in one direction, like many sweater knits. Double knits are basically two single knits back to back, so they will not roll; and often, both sides look identical. Double knits have become so sophisticated in design that some of them even look like woven fabric. Because knits are made from a continuous series of loops, most of them stretch in all directions and do not ravel. The most stretch is found when the fabric is pulled on the crosswise grain, perpendicular to the finished edges called the selvage (figure 3-4). Although woven and knit fabrics differ from one another in many ways, all washable fabrics should be preshrunk before cutting out a project.

Years ago we were taught to preshrink fabric because we could expect a lot of shrinkage which greatly altered the fit after the

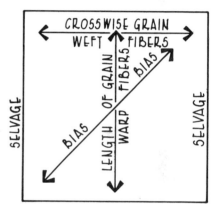

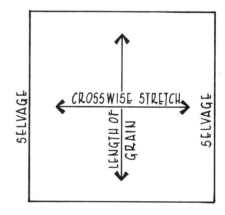

Figure 3-4 Characteristics of woven fabric and knit fabric.

Figure 3-3 A sewing organizer and some supplies.

garment was first washed. Fabric manufacturers have solved most of the shrinkage problems of natural and synthetic fibers, but it is still important to preshrink fabric before sewing. Many of today's fabrics have an invisible finish, called *sizing*, that adds extra body to make the fabrics look and feel good on the bolt. This chemical finish can build up on your sewing machine needle and cause skipped stitches. Preshrink your fabric in the manner you plan to care for the garment after it is finished. While preshrinking the fashion fabric, preshrink other notions you will be using in the project, such as lining, zipper, trim, and seam binding. But do not get carried away. One home sewer preshrunk her fabric, notions, and her fusible (iron-on) interfacing. She then threw everything in the dryer, including the interfacing, which melted and fused everything into one big mess.

INTERFACING

Interfacing is an added piece of inner fabric used in garment construction to firm up stress areas and to give body and shaping to a garment at the neckline and armhole areas, collars, cuffs, front openings, etc. When used properly, interfacing makes the difference between a project looking homemade and one that looks ready-to-wear. Interfacing comes in many weights and types for different kinds of fashion fabrics. Interfacing may be woven, knitted, or formed fabric, which is actually fibers that have been

pressed together like felt. Some interfacing is fusible, having been coated with a heat-sensitive adhesive on one side. Check your favorite fabric store to choose the proper interfacing for your project. Many companies indicate the uses and types of fabrics the interfacing is suitable for on the bolt hangtag, or on a plastic film that is wrapped with the interfacing. I happen to be a fan of fusible interfacing, because it stays in place and is easy to work with.

Fusible interfacing: While your pattern instruction sheet will tell you how to use sew-in interfacings, there are three ingredients necessary for fusible interfacing to permanently adhere it to the fashion fabric—heat, moisture, and pressure. To be safe, test a small piece of the fusible interfacing on your fabric first.

Cut interfacing ¼-inch (6mm.) smaller all the way around than the fashion-fabric pattern piece. With the tip of a hot iron, heat baste interfacing in two or three places around the edges. Be sure the fusible side is against the wrong side of the fashion fabric. This insures correct placement and also prevents fusing the interfacing to your iron instead of the fabric.

Wet a press cloth until it is almost dripping wet and place it over your work. With a very hot iron (cotton setting), firmly press until all the moisture has evaporated. Do not slide the iron— lift and press until the entire piece is fused. This insures a permanent bond for very professional results.

NOTIONS

A general rule to follow when selecting sewing notions is to coordinate the fiber content of fabric and notions as closely as possible. If you are sewing cotton, use cotton thread, zipper, tapes, and trims. If you are sewing nylon fabric, use nylon thread, zipper, tapes, and trims. Also select sewing notions of a weight similar to that of the fabric. For instance, when sewing lightweight fabrics, use a fine needle, fine thread, lightweight interfacing and zipper. For heavier fabrics, use a heavier needle, a slightly heavier thread, heavier interfacing and zipper. Threads with a fiber content similar to your fabric may be hard to find; so you will have to use those most compatible with your fashion fabric.

I prefer to use 100 percent cotton mercerized thread on some projects because it has excellent luster and will not cause uneven thread tensions. If you find that cotton thread frays or piles up behind the eye of the needle, put it in the refrigerator overnight. Moisture will be absorbed into the thread. It then regains its original tensile strength without shrinking.

To simplify your thread purchase, thread companies make products that work well on most fabrics. There are differences from brand to brand. Try all of them to find what works best with your machine. The most widely available thread for the home sewer is cotton-wrapped polyester. Because the polyester core of this thread stretches more than all-cotton thread, you may have to loosen sewing machine tensions slightly to prevent puckered seams.

Another common thread type is 100 percent spun polyester. The quality polyester threads are made from long fibers which give the thread a smooth, even appearance. It is often available in two weights—one weight for general sewing and a heavier weight for tailored topstitching. In either case, you may have to loosen sewing machine tensions for smooth, unpuckered seams.

Other thread types include nylon, used for sewing lingerie, outdoor parkas, backpacks, etc.; rayon made especially for machine embroidery; and silk for sewing fine woolens and silks. When choosing thread, do not be duped into buying the bargain variety. Cheap thread is no bar-

gain if it results in tension problems, puckered seams, and uneven stitching.

NEEDLES

Change your sewing machine needle once a garment. A new needle is the best way to prevent skipped stitches, snagging, and puckered seams. I am often reminded of the woman who complained to me that her machine would not stay threaded. Upon closer inspection, I discovered she had worn the needle down to the eye!

To replace the needle, find the flat side of the thick part, or needle shaft (figure 3-5). For machines with side-loading bobbins, the flat side of the needle faces the right. For machines with top- or front-loading bobbins, the flat side of the needle faces the back of the machine. Be sure the nee-

dle is all the way up into the needle clamp before tightening the screw. You may want to tighten the needle-clamp screw with a screwdriver so the needle will not loosen or fall out while sewing.

Needle Selection

Woven fabrics have been sewn for years using *sharp needles*. With the introduction of knit fabrics, the sharp needle often snagged the fabric and caused skipped stitches. To solve this problem, needle manufacturers developed the *ball-point needle* with a rounded tip that slides through the loops of the knit without damage to the fabric. That meant the home sewer had to keep a supply of ball-point needles on hand for sewing knits, and a supply of sharp needles for wovens. Needle manufacturers

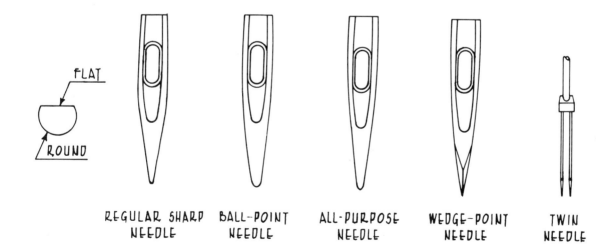

REGULAR SHARP NEEDLE   BALL-POINT NEEDLE   ALL-PURPOSE NEEDLE   WEDGE-POINT NEEDLE   TWIN NEEDLE

Figure 3-5 Sewing machine needles.

type of fabric		machine needles			thread	
		U. S. Size 15 x 1	Eur. Size 130/705	Style	Mercerized Cotton	Cotton-covered Polyester
KNITS	LIGHTWEIGHT Tricot	White Golden Ball 11	70H	All-Purpose	YES	YES
	MEDIUM WEIGHT Interlock, Qiana, Swimsuit fabric, Power Net (Spandex)	Super Needle 14	75 - 90 H - S	Stretch	YES	YES
	HEAVYWEIGHT Double Knit, Velours	White Golden Ball 14	80 - 90 H	All-Purpose	YES	YES
	FAKE FURS & FURLIKE FABRICS	White Golden Ball 14	90 - 100 H	All-Purpose	YES	YES
WOVENS	VERY SHEER Lace, Net, Chiffon, Voile	9	60 H	All-Purpose	YES	YES
	SHEER Qiana, Lawn, Taffeta, Gingham, Crepe, Organdy	9	70 H	All-Purpose	YES	YES
	MEDIUM - Wool, Linen, Piqué, Brocade, Velvet, Velveteen, Terrycloth, Nylon (outer wear)	11	80 H	All-Purpose	YES	YES
	HEAVY Denim, Corduroy, Sailcloth, Duck	14	90 H - J	Sharp	YES	YES
	EXTRA HEAVY Canvas, Upholstery, Awning, Drapery Fabric	14 - 16	90 H - J or 90 - 110	Sharp or All-Purpose	YES	YES
LEATHER	VINYLS	Leather 16	NTW 90 - 110	Wedge-point	YES	YES
	LIGHT TO MEDIUM WEIGHT Leathers & Suedes	Leather 14	NTW 90	Wedge-point	YES	YES
	FURLIKE FABRIC WITH VINYL BACKING	Leather 16	NTW 90 - 100	Wedge-point	YES	YES
	HEAVY	Leather 16	NTW 90 - 100	Wedge-point	YES	YES
DECORATIVE STITCHING	MACHINE EMBROIDERY	Golden Ball 11 & 14	80 - 90 H	All-purpose	YES	NO
	TOPSTITCHING WITH HEAVIER THREAD	14 - 16	Topstitching 90	All-purpose Large Eye	NO	NO
	TWIN NEEDLES	Dist btwn. needles 2.0mm 2.0mm 2.7mm 2.7mm 4.0mm	Size U. S. Eur. 10/70 12/80 12/80 14/90 16/100	All-purpose		

Figure 3-6 Needle, thread, fabric, and stitching guide.

Polyester	Nylon	**presser feet**
NO	YES	Teflon/Metal
NO	YES	Teflon/Metal
YES	NO	Teflon/Metal
YES	NO	Roller Foot
NO	YES	Teflon/Metal
NO	NO	Teflon/Metal
NO	NO	Teflon/Metal
YES	NO	Teflon/Metal
YES	NO	Teflon/Metal
YES	NO	Roller Foot
YES	NO	Roller Foot
YES	NO	Roller Foot
YES	NO	Roller Foot
NO	NO	Varies/Embroidery
YES	NO	Teflon/Metal
		Embroidery/Pin Tuck Foot

recognized the confusion and developed *all-purpose needles* in many sizes for most types and weights of fabric. However, the all-purpose needle does not solve the sewing problems created by speciality fabrics or special types of sewing, such as embroidery and decorative stitching.

Speciality Needles

There are needles for practically every purpose imaginable, all of which make it easier to achieve professional results.

Wedge-point needle: Many home sewers are beginning to sew outerwear made of leather, leatherlike, suedelike, or vinyl fabrics. For these projects, a wedge-point needle is recommended. The point is knifelike. It slices into the leather or vinyl rather than perforating the seam like other needles. This needle is usually available in three sizes: 11, 14, and 16 (American needle sizing), or 90, 100, 110 (European needle sizing). Test for the proper size, starting with the finest needle first.

Twin needle: Another needle type designed for decorative stitching and pin tucking is the twin needle. It has two needles that share a common shaft and works only on top- or front-loading bobbin sewing machines. For more sewing information on using the twin needle, see pages 124–126 and 134.

Stretch needle: Recently, fabrics called *interlock knits* were introduced to the home-sewing market. This type of fabric is beautiful, drapeable, and comes in bright prints and brilliant colors. Unfortunately, the yarns can run like pantyhose yarns and have a tendency to cause skipped stitches. Needle manufacturers came up with the stretch needle, available in two sizes, 11 and 14 (American needle sizing), or 75 and 90 (European needle sizing). The needle itself is sometimes blue in color which helps make it stand out from the all-purpose needles.

The stretch needle virtually solves skipped stitches, but should only be used when the all-purpose needle fails. The reason behind this is that the stretch needle is positioned closer to the hook in the race area than other needles. If the fabric is stretched while being sewn, it can be pulled into the hook and break.

Denim needle: The denim needle was designed for use in sewing, recycling, and repairing denim; sewing upholstery; or working on heavy nylon outerwear for duffle bags, sleeping bags, and tenting. The needle is very sharp and available in limited sizes. Unlike the wedge-point needle that cuts through the fabric, the denim needle separates densely woven fibers, preventing fabric damage.

Topstitching needle: If you enjoy tailored detail, there is a needle to make topstitching easy. It has an elongated eye to better accommodate polyester topstitching and similar threads, or multiple threads through the eye. *Note:* For quick reference, consult the Needle, Thread, Fabric, and Stitching Guide (figure 3-6).

SCISSORS AND SHEARS

No matter how carefully you laid out your pattern, the accuracy of the stitching line will be only as accurate as the cutting line. For an accurate cutting line, pin pattern on the fabric, using a lot of pins or pattern weights, and cut out the project with a sharp pair of shears.

There are many brands of scissors and shears available for every sewing need. If you choose your shears carefully, you should not have to replace them very often. There are two basic types of shears, classified by what they are made from. Heavy shears are built of hot-forged steel and are hardened for a sharp edge. Lightweight shears are made of an aluminum alloy. Both have their advantages. Find the type that suits your hand and needs the best.

The hot-forged steel shears tend to be heavy and a bit clumsy to work with but can be resharpened many times and may outlast the lightweight shears.

The lightweight shears are comfortable, but some brands cannot be easily sharpened. I recently used a pair of lightweight shears that can be resharpened, because the blades are joined with a screw instead of a rivet. The comfortable handle is bent at an extra high angle for an accurate cutting line (figure 3-7).

If alterations are not necessary, and the fabric will not easily ravel, speed up the cutting process and *do not* cut the pointed notches indicated on the pattern piece. Instead, use sharp scissor points and clip in a ⅛-inch (3mm.) slit into the seam allowance at every notch. A single notch is made with one clip, a double notch with two, etc. Besides saving time, the notch clips are more accurate, and there are no notches to be trimmed off the seam allowance before pressing a seam. *Note:* If you fit your garment as you sew, cut around the notches, as you may need all the fabric in the seam allowance.

PATTERN SELECTION AND LAYOUT

After the fabrics and notions are prepared, it is time for the pattern layout. Be sure you have chosen the right pattern for your fashion fabric. Always consult your pattern envelope for recommended fabrics for a particular pattern. It will indicate whether a knit or woven fabric is best.

Woven fabrics require a pattern that calls for more fitting—more darts, gathers, and seams. Knits, however, do not present as many fitting problems as woven fabrics, but they stretch in varying degrees and require different pattern selections and construction techniques. When selecting a knit fabric use this guide:

If 4 inches (10cm.) of knit fabric, stretched on the cross grain stretches ½-inch (1.3cm.) or less, you can use this fabric with patterns that call for woven fabrics. This knit is relatively stable, is handled like a woven fabric, and requires more fitting than other knit fabrics.

If 4 inches (10cm.) of knit

Figure 3-7 Shears.

fabric stretched on the cross grain stretches ½-inch (1.3cm.) to 2 inches (5cm.), use it only with patterns marked *for stretchable unbonded knits only.* These patterns are designed with less fitting requirements and the style is usually very simple.

If 4 inches (10cm.) of knit fabric stretched on the cross grain stretches more than 2 inches (5cm.), you should use one of the patterns for knits only. These patterns usually have several sizes included in one pattern. Therefore, the proper size has to be traced onto a large piece of tissue paper or tracing fabric. Seam allowances are usually ¼-inch (6mm.) for this type of pattern, and instructions include shortcuts that are easy to understand.

After the pattern and fabric have been selected, you are ready to lay out your pattern on the fabric. Pattern pieces are marked with an arrow and must be placed on the *straight of the grain* (see page 29). The straight of the grain is parallel with the finished selvage edge. Always check layout instructions included on your pattern instruction sheet for accurate information.

When laying out a pattern on a knit fabric, pattern pieces should be cut using a *with nap* layout. Even though most knits are not considered napped fabrics, if pieces are cut in different directions, the garment may look like it is two different colors. Pattern pieces must also be cut with the most stretch going around the body. If the garment is cut in the other direction, it will grow in length and will not fit properly.

Matching a Plaid or Stripe

Use the notches marked on your pattern as a guide wherever possible. Notches marked like this: ▲, ▲▲, ▲, on a pattern piece, are numbered and show where two pattern pieces are to be lined up and sewn together. If, for example, notch #11 on one pattern piece is even with a yellow stripe or bar in a plaid, then notch #11 on the corresponding pattern piece should also be even with the yellow stripe or bar so both pattern pieces will match. For a better point of reference, trace the plaid or stripe directly on the tissue pattern piece to indicate the repeat in the design. Match this piece to the fabric, then place the corresponding pattern on the fabric, matching markings. Always be sure to match pieces at the seam lines, not the cutting lines. Important areas to be matched are: center fronts, side fronts, side seams, center backs, and if possible, sleeves and armholes at the front.

Chapter 4

IMPORTANT PREPARATIONS

Remember the Golden Rule of sewing: "As ye sew, so must ye rip." The time spent marking and basting your project together may save time later on.

Before I discuss stitch settings, let me establish a standard to use throughout the book to understand the difference between stitch length and stitch width.

STITCH LENGTH

Stitch length is the main control on any sewing machine. It determines the distance the feed dog moves the fabric under the needle and presser foot. The longer the stitch length, the further the feed dog must move the fabric for each stitch. Many older machines have the stitch length control set by the number of stitches per inch. The *higher* the number, the *shorter* the stitch (12 stitches per inch is a shorter stitch than 6 stitches per inch). Many modern sewing machines, however, have the stitch length measured in millimeters (mm.), making the opposite ratio true: the *higher* the number, the *longer* the stitch. For example, a "1" stitch length equals a stitch that is 1mm. long, a "2" stitch length equals a stitch that is 2mm. long, etc. Most machines have a maximum stitch length of 4mm. to 5mm. (equal to about 3/16-inch without the use of a basting or topstitching accessory (figure 4-1).

Test for the proper stitch length on a scrap of fabric using the following guidelines:

If the fabric puckers as you sew, shorten the stitch length. By shortening the stitch, more thread is sewn in the seam, the fabric relaxes, and puckering is eliminated. This occurs most often with lightweight fabrics.

If the fabric ripples out of shape as you sew, lengthen the stitch. By lengthening the stitch, less thread is used in the seam, preventing a lot of thread and stitches from pushing the fabric out of shape. This is a problem mainly with loosely woven and extremely stretchy knit fabrics such as velour and stretch terry cloth.

STITCH WIDTH

The stitch width, found on zig-zag and reverse-action machines, controls the needle swing from side to side. It is generally marked from 0 to 4, meaning the stitch can be from 0 to 4 millimeters (mm.). When the stitch width control is set on "1", the width control is set on "1", the needle swings side to side forming a stitch 1mm. wide. The higher the number, the wider the stitch. The widest stitch is generally 4 to 5 mm., and in some cases as wide as 7 mm. (figure 4-1).

STITCH STANDARDIZATION

For easy reference in this book, stitch length and width settings are described from 0 to 4. Zero means no stitch length and/or no stitch width. Four means the longest and/or widest stitch (see figure 4-1 to convert stitches per inch into millimeters).

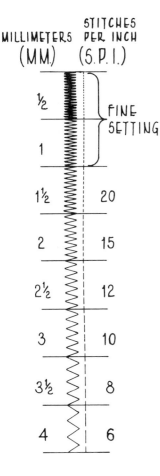

Figure 4-1 Millimeters versus stitches per inch.

MARKING YOUR PATTERN PIECES BY HAND

There are many different ways to transfer pattern markings to your fabric. Which method you choose depends on what kind of fabric you are using and the amount of time you want to spend.

Hand Tailor Tacks

Hand tailor tacks are the most accurate and should be sewn with a single strand of slightly contrasting-color thread. Mercerized cotton or basting thread are good choices.

1. Thread your needle with about 18 inches (46cm.) of thread, leaving the end unknotted.

2. Take a stitch through the pattern and both layers of fabric, leaving a thread tail about 1-inch (2.5cm.) long. Take another stitch at the same point, leaving a loop approximately ¾-inch (18mm.) long (figure 4-2).

3. Cut thread at the needle end, about 1 inch (2.5cm.) from fashion fabric.

4. Carefully pull the pattern tissue off fashion fabric. Separate the two layers of fabric until there is a resistance to the thread tacks.

5. Clip threads between layers of fabric. The fabric is now accurately marked (figure 4-3).

Although tailor tacks are quite accurate, they can be time-consuming. How do you get the accuracy of hand tailor tacks

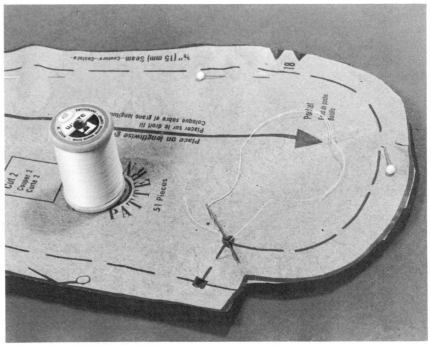

Figure 4-2 A hand-tailored tack.

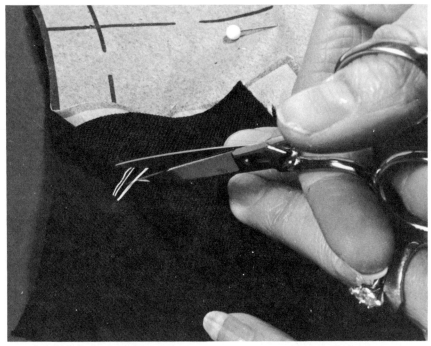

Figure 4-3 Clipping a tailor tack.

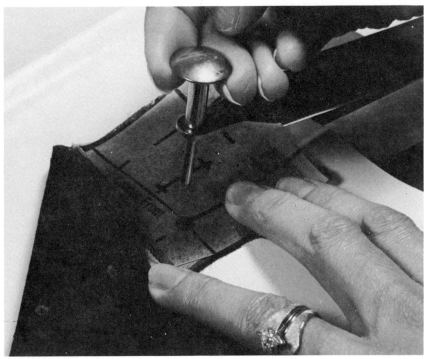

Figure 4-4 Using Tack-It.

without wasting a lot of time? Try one of the following methods:

Tack-It

This gadget makes marking pattern pieces a snap.

1. Fold a piece of dressmaker's tracing paper in half with the right side on the outside (be sure to use tracing paper that is washable).

2. Place tracing paper between the two layers of fabric where the marking is going to be done. Make sure the marks will be made on the wrong side of the fabric.

3. Place the fabric with tracing paper and tissue pattern piece under the Tack-It at the point the pattern is to be marked. Pull up on the knob then let go. The marker strikes the pattern piece without damaging the tissue pattern and makes a visible mark on the fabric as accurately as hand tailor tacks, without the bother (figure 4-4). *Note:* This method works beautifully to mark dark fabrics when you use a light-colored tracing paper.

Bar of Soap

Use the straight edge of an old bar of soap to mark hemlines, buttonholes, or pocket placement. It works well on dark, washable fabrics, and can be used on both right and wrong sides of the fabric. Remember to test soap marks on fashion fabric to be sure they will not leave grease spots when the garment is pressed. To remove the marks just wash the garment.

Felt-tip Fabric Marker

Another accurate way to mark a pattern is with a felt-tip fabric-marking pen. Many brands are available, including one with purple ink that automatically disappears after forty-eight hours. It is great for marking pattern pieces and for transferring embroidery or quilting designs to a *dry-clean only* piece of fabric.

After the garment has been cut out, mark darts, pleats, tucks, etc. by pressing firmly with the pen directly on the pattern tissue wherever a mark is to be made. The ink bleeds through the tissue pattern, the top layer of fabric, and finally to the second layer of fabric. Be careful to double-check that the ink has bled through to the second layer of fabric before removing the tissue pattern. When using this technique, mark pattern pieces as you sew. Then you do not run the risk of the mark disappearing before you get to it.

Cellophane Tape

Cellophane tape comes in handy for many things, especially for marking darts and for zipper insertions. Test the tape on your fabric first to make sure it will come off easily and not harm your fabric. Avoid sewing over the tape, as the adhesive could stick to your needle and cause skipped stitches.

Use the long edge of the tape as a stitching guide and sew from the widest part of the dart to the point (figure 4-5). Remove tape before pressing. Tape is also useful as a stitching guide or tem-plate for the final stitching on a zipper application. (See page 57 for information on zipper insertions.)

Also use the tape as a stitching guide for topstitching, marking buttonhole length, and instead of pins to hold hems in place.

Pin Marking

You can also transfer pattern markings to fashion fabric using pins.

1. At a dot or square, simply pin straight through the pattern tissue and both fabric layers, pushing pin in up to the head. This pin marks one pattern piece.
2. From the other side of the pattern piece, push another pin straight through both fabric layers and pattern tissue, up to the head. This pin marks the other pattern piece.
3. Carefully pull pattern tissue off fashion fabric, pulling pin heads through the tissue.
4. Finally, pull both fabric layers apart. The pin heads pull up to the fabric, and the pattern pieces are marked.

Before I leave the subject of marking and basting, you should be aware of a double-sided basting tape used for trim placement, holding zippers in place for stitching, and basting hems and seams on leather, vinyl, suede, and suedelike synthetics. Just another way to save home sewers more time.

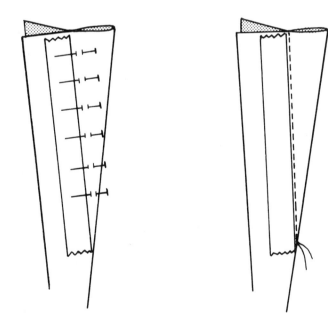

Figure 4-5 Marking and stitching a dart.

Figure 4-6 Machine-tailored tacks.

Figure 4-7 Machine basting with thin-material foot.

MARKING PATTERN PIECES BY MACHINE

A way to mark a pattern piece with your zigzag or reverse-action sewing machine is with a zigzag stitch and a *fringe* or *looping foot* (page 23). This accessory is available at your local dealer for most sewing machine models and can be used to accurately mark your pattern pieces as well as for other decorative purposes.

Stitch: . . . . Zigzag stitch
Foot: . . . . Fringe foot
Stitch length: . . 2 to 3mm. or 10 to 15 stitches per inch
Stitch width: . . 4mm.

1. Loosen upper tension.
2. Place fabric and pattern pieces together under fringe foot.
3. Using the zigzag stitch, mark desired lines with stitching. The stitch will look like loose chenille that stands away from the fabric (figure 4-6).
4. After stitching is complete, remove perforated tissue pattern and pull the fabric pieces apart until there is resistance to the stitch.
5. Cut the threads joining fabric. Machine tacks are made.

MACHINE BASTING

Easy basting can be done with all three types of sewing machines.

Straight-Stitch Sewing Machine

Although the straight-stitch foot will work for machine basting, a *walking* or thin-material foot (page 23) helps prevent seams from puckering, which often happens when a long stitch is used, especially on a fine fabric (figure 4-7).

Stitch: . . . . Straight stitch
Foot: . . . . Thin-material foot or straight-stitch foot
Stitch length: . . 3 to 4mm. or 6 to 10 stitches per inch

1. Loosen upper tension slightly; this allows the stitching to be pulled out easily.

2. Machine baste seams on the seamline to properly fit the garment (figure 4-7). After you have completed all fitting and basting, return the upper tension to its normal setting and stitch seams.

3. After the final stitching of the seam, pull bobbin thread of the basting stitches for easy removal. *Hint:* You may want to use a different color bobbin thread for basting so you can easily see which thread to pull out after the final stitching.

4. Return upper tension to normal setting.

Zigzag Sewing Machine

Stitch: . . . . Zigzag stitch
Foot: . . . . Zigzag or embroidery foot
Stitch length: . . 3 to 4mm. or 6 to 10 stitches per inch
Stitch width: . . 4mm.

1. Loosen upper tension.

2. Using the zigzag stitch pre-viously indicated, machine baste on seamline (figure 4-8).

3. Press the seam lightly, then fit the garment. Return the upper tension to its normal setting and stitch seams.

4. After the final stitching, pull the bobbin thread of machine basting. The stitches come out quickly and easily. Return upper tension to normal setting.

Reverse-Action Sewing Machine

Each machine manufacturer usually has a basting accessory available for their machines.

Some brands use a short *Free Westinghouse* needle, available through local sewing machine sales and service centers. Other machines use a double-eyed needle or have basting accessories or features built in. Most machines that are designed to use a basting accessory skip every other stitch; so basting stitches are approximately ¼-inch (6mm.)–½-inch (12mm.) long.

Stitch: . . . . Zigzag stitch
Foot: . . . . Zigzag foot
Stitch length: . . 4mm. or 6 stitches per inch
Stitch width: . . 4mm.

Figure 4-8 Machine basting with zigzag stitch.

Figure 4-9 Machine basting with accessory.

1. Loosen upper tension slightly.

2. Using the basting accessory designed for your machine, such as the one in figure 4-9, baste on seamline to properly fit the garment. Return the upper tension to its normal setting, and stitch seams.

3. After final stitching, pull bobbin thread of the basting stitch. *Hint:* This long basting stitch can also be sewn with silk twist or polyester topstitching thread for a decorative *saddle stitch* on tailored suits and sportswear.

4. Return upper tension to normal setting.

Chapter 5

SHORTCUTS FROM NECKLINE TO HEMLINE

I have always maintained that anyone who sews must be a person with vision. First of all, we choose a pattern without knowing if it will fit. We often choose fabric without knowing what it is going to be used for, if it will shrink, if the color will fade, or if the finished garment will last long enough to hand down to someone else. We make an outfit without knowing what it will look like when it is finished, and we sew on machines without knowing what makes them tick. We do not want to appear to ourselves, or others, as having that homemade look.

Ways *not* to look homemade are to take care in pressing every seam and learning the professional shortcuts discussed in this chapter. Let's begin with pressing.

I would like to amend the sewer's Golden Rule to: "As ye sew, so must ye rip...and *press.*" Notice the word is *press,* not *iron.* Ironing is when the iron is pushed back and forth, resulting in a shiny finish on the seams and pocket flaps, and stretched-out shoulder seams, etc., because the iron is pushing and polishing the fibers.

Pressing, on the other hand, means that an iron or commercial press is placed over a seam, and the heat, pressure, and moisture press a seam, pocket flap, etc., without a shine or ridge. When using a hand iron, place it on the seam and press in one spot for a few seconds. Pick it up, and set the iron down in another spot until the seam is pressed. Care must be taken when pressing quality fabrics because they often require the use of a damp press cloth. *Hint:* It is a good idea to get in the habit of always using a press cloth when you sew.

A press cloth should be made of a fiber that can withstand high temperatures—cotton or wool work well. There are also disposable press cloths that are chemically treated to be used with extreme heat. This type of press cloth holds water well when you need extra moisture and is great for fusing interfacing because it is translucent. You can see the interfacing in place, and any chemical residue from the interfacing comes off on the press cloth, not on your iron or ironing board. But, before we can start pressing, we must sew something. Let us start with a straight seam.

A straight seam is made by joining two pieces of fabric with a row of stitching. To join two pieces of fabric, fabric pieces must be pinned and/or basted together before final stitching of the seam. Regardless of what the salesman told you when you bought your machine, remove the pins before sewing over them. This way you avoid breaking a needle, and you have a much safer sewing experience. Traditionally, seam allowances have been ⅝-inch (15mm.) wide, measuring from the raw edge to the stitching line. The seam allowance must be wide enough to insure the fabric will not ravel up to the stitching line and to allow enough fabric for fitting. In most cases, raw woven fabric edges must be finished off either by *pinking* the edge with pinking shears, using a binding, or by overcasting the seam with a row of machine stitching. For knits, it is best to use narrow seams as described on page 48.

SEAM FINISHES FOR STRAIGHT SEAMS ON WOVEN FABRICS

Traditionally, seam finishes have been sewn *after* garment construction. Before the advent of zigzag and reverse-action stitches, seam finishes sewn with a straight-stitch machine eliminated fabric from the seam allowance. This drastically altered the fit of the finished garment.

Although finishing seams after construction is still recommended for those of you with straight-stitch sewing machines, it is often difficult because the fabric has raveled or the seam allowance is in a hard-to-finish area. The following seam-finish-ing techniques for zigzag and reverse-action sewing machines are recommended *before* garment construction. The stitch and presser feet used in these techniques prevent raw fabric edges from tunneling under the stitch and you are, therefore, assured of an accurate ⅝-inch (15mm.) seam allowance.

Straight-Stitch Sewing Machine

A straight-stitch sewing machine can be used to professionally finish seams by sewing a clean-finished edge, using the bias binder, or by stitching close to a pinked edge.

Clean-finished Edge

Stitch: . . . . Straight stitch
Foot: . . . . Straight-stitch
            foot
Stitch length:. . 2 to 3mm. or 10
            to 15 stitches per
            inch

1. After seam is stitched, turn one raw edge under ⅛-inch (3mm.) and press.
2. Stitch very close to folded edge (figure 5-1A).
3. Repeat for other seam allowances.
4. Carefully press seam open, placing strips of brown paper between seam allowance and body of the garment. This will prevent the seam allowance from marking the right side of the garment while pressing.

Stitched and Pinked Finish

Stitch: . . . . Straight stitch
Foot: . . . . Straight-stitch
            foot

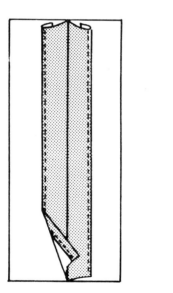

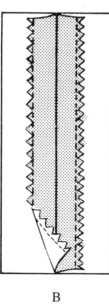

A   B

Figure 5-1 Clean-finished edge (left) and stitched and pinked edge (right).

Stitch length: .. 2mm. or 15 stitches per inch

1. Cut project out with a sharp *straight* pair of shears. *Note:* Never cut a garment out with pinking shears. You will get an inaccurate cutting line.

2. After final stitching of each seam, trim or pink one raw edge at a time with pinking shears.

3. Run a line of straight stitching about ⅛-inch (3mm.) from pinked edge for a clean, professional finish (figure 5-1B).

4. Press seam open.

Bias Binder

A bias binder simplifies seam finishes on garments, crafts, and household gift items. Binders are available through your local sewing machine dealer and also fit zigzag and reverse-action sewing machines.

Stitch: .... Straight stitch
Foot: .... Bias-binder foot
Stitch length: .. 2 to 3mm. or 10 to 15 stitches per inch

1. After seam is stitched, place the bias-binder attachment on the machine.

2. Using a single-fold bias tape, or bias-cut strip approximately ¾-inch (18mm.) wide, cut a V on the end of the tape.

3. Thread the tape through the cone-shaped feeder.

4. Place the raw fabric edge into the binder, stitching the bias tape on the fabric (figure 5-2). *Hint:* When turning a corner, shorten the stitch length.

5. Carefully press seam open, placing strips of brown paper between the seam allowance and the body of the garment. This will prevent the seam allowance from marking the right side of the garment while pressing.

Zigzag Sewing Machines

Method 1

The zigzag stitch is a natural choice for a fast seam finish. It is much easier to use than the bias binder or pinking shears because the seam is finished before garment construction.

Stitch: .... Zigzag stitch
Foot: .... Overcast guide-foot
Stitch length: .. 1 to 2mm. or fine setting to 15 stitches per inch
Stitch width: .. 4mm.

1. Place raw fabric edge halfway under the presser foot so the needle bites into the fabric at the left and swings off the raw edge on the right (figure 5-3). *Note:* Using the overcast guide-foot keeps fabric edges from curling or tunneling under the stitch, and guarantees an accurate stitching line.

2. Baste and fit garment as needed.

3. Pin fabric pieces with right sides together and sew a seam with a straight stitch on the ⅝-inch (15mm.) seamline.

4. Press finished seam open.

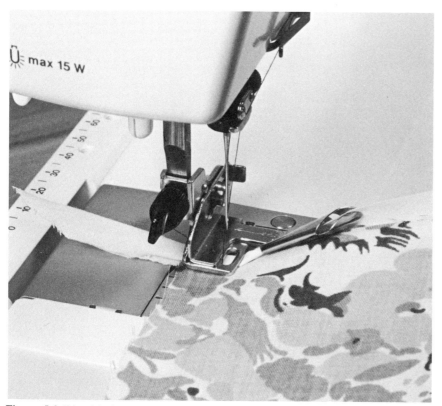

Figure 5-2 Bias binder.

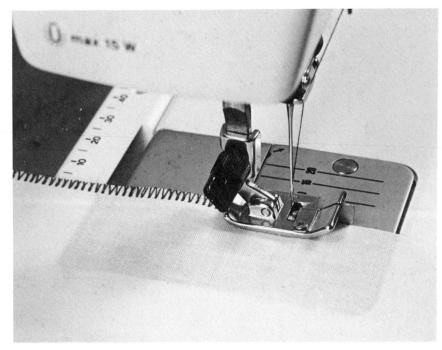

Figure 5-3 Overcasting with a zigzag stitch.

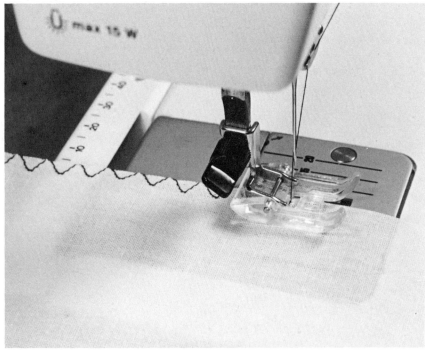

Figure 5-4 Overcasting with a multiple-zigzag stitch.

Method 2

Although the zigzag stitch is satisfactory for finishing seams, the multiple-zigzag stitch is a better choice because it will give a smoother, flatter seam finish. *Note:* The standard zigzag or embroidery foot can be used for this seam finish because the stitch itself is designed to prevent fabric edges from tunneling under the stitch.

Stitch: . . . . Multiple-zigzag stitch
Foot: . . . . Zigzag or embroidery foot
Stitch length: . . 1mm. or fine setting
Stitch width: . . 4mm.

1. Place the raw fabric edge under the pressure foot. Guide the fabric so the needle takes short stitches from side to side, the last stitch on the right swings off the raw edge (figure 5-4).
2. Baste and fit garment as needed.
3. Pin fabric pieces with right sides together and sew with a straight stitch on the ⅝-inch (15mm.) seamline.
4. Press finished seam open (figure 5-5).

Reverse-Action Sewing Machine

I love it when someone asks me where I bought my outfit, and I can answer with pride, "I made it!" Although previously discussed techniques are acceptable seam finishes, reverse-action stitches give a more professional look to handmade garments and can be used on a wider variety of both woven and knit fabrics.

Seam allowances can be overcast with a number of different reverse-action stitches. Always test the stitch before using it to be sure it is compatible with the fabric you are working with.

Method 1

The overlock stitch is excellent for overcasting ravel-prone woven fabrics and for seaming lightweight woven and knit fabrics. For woven fabrics, such as gabardine, corduroy, denim, etc., overcast raw edges *before* the garment is constructed (figure 5-5).

Stitch: . . . . Overlock stitch
Foot: . . . . Embroidery or overcast guide-foot
Stitch length: . . Stretch-stitch or cam setting
Stitch width: . . 4mm.

Method 2

The double overlock stitch is recommended for medium to heavy woven fabrics that ravel, such as wool flannel and raw silk. The double overlock stitch is excellent for seams and edge finishes on Qiana and medium weight jersey and interlock knits. It may also be used for the inside-out topstitched look on jeans, T-shirts, and other sportswear.

For very ravel-prone fabrics, overcast raw edges *before* the garment is constructed (figure 5-6).

Stitch: . . . . Double overlock stitch
Foot: . . . . Zigzag or overcast guide-foot
Stitch length: . . Stretch-stitch or cam setting
Stitch width: . . 3 to 4mm.

Method 3

The super-stretch stitch was originally designed for use on extremely stretchy fabrics, such as sweater knits and swimsuit fabrics, because it has a memory built into it. However, it can also be used to overcast raw edges on woven fabrics (fabric 5-6).

Stitch: . . . . Super-stretch stitch
Foot: . . . . Zigzag or embroidery foot
Stitch length: . . Stretch-stitch or cam setting
Stitch width: . . 4mm.

Figure 5-6 Overcasting with a reverse-action stitch.

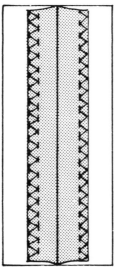

Figure 5-5 Pressed ⅝-inch seams.

47

KNIT SEAMS AND SEAM FINISHES

Quarter-inch (6mm.) seams are common in knit ready-to-wear garments because ⅝-inch (15mm.) seams are often bulky, curl, and have a raw appearance in the finished garment. You can achieve the same professional results by stitching ¼-inch (6mm.) seams in your handmade knitwear.

Knit seams can be sewn on the ⅝-inch (15mm.) seamline, then trimmed to ¼-inch (6mm.). However, to make your sewing even faster, choose a pattern that calls for ¼-inch (6mm.), rather than ⅝-inch (15mm.) seams so you do not waste time trimming the extra seam allowance. If you are using a pattern that needs little or no alteration, trim seam allowances to ¼-inch (6mm.) when you are cutting out the garment.

No matter what type of knit you are working with, narrow seams must be sewn and/or finished to insure a durable seam, comfortable fit, and to prevent unnecessary bulk in the seams. The weight of the fabric determines what stitch should be used. The following methods should be test-sewn on fabric scraps before final stitching of the project. This way, you can be sure that the garment fits and that the seam finish is compatible with the fabric you are working on.

The following methods are recommended for velour, stretch terry cloth, sweater knits, and double knits. These medium to heavy knit fabrics should be sewn with ¼-inch (6mm.) seams.

Straight-Stitch Sewing Machine

Stitch: . . . . Straight stitch
Foot: . . . . Straight-stitch foot
Stitch length: . . 2 to 2½mm. or 12 to 15 stitches per inch

1. Pin fabric pieces with right sides together.
2. Using the edge of the presser foot as a guide, begin sewing the seam ¼-inch (6mm.) from the raw edge. *Note:* By using 100 percent polyester thread, the seams will stretch and give with the garment.
3. After the first row of stitching is complete, stitch a second row next to the first ⅛-inch (3mm.) from the raw edge.
4. Press the seam to one side. *Hint:* To stabilize the seam, stitch over a piece of ¼-inch (6mm.) twill tape.

Zigzag Sewing Machine

Step 1:

Stitch: . . . . Zigzag stitch
Foot: . . . . Zigzag or embroidery foot
Stitch length: . . 1 to 2mm. or fine setting to 15 stitches per inch
Stitch width: . . 1mm.

1. Pin fabric pieces with right sides together.
2. Using a tiny zigzag stitch, sew the seam ¼-inch (6mm.) from the raw edge. The zigzag stitch will stretch with the garment without having to stretch the fabric as you sew.

Step 2:

Stitch: . . . . Multiple-zigzag stitch
Foot: . . . . Zigzag or embroidery foot
Stitch length: . . 1mm. or fine setting
Stitch width: . . 4mm.

1. Place the seam sewn in Step 1 under the foot so the needle stitches next to the first row of stitching on the left. The multiple-zigzag stitch stretches with the seam and flattens the seam allowance (figure 5-7).
2. Trim excess seam allowance.
3. Press finished seam to one side.

Reverse-Action Sewing Machine

This technique saves a lot of time because the seam is stitched and finished in one step.

Stitch Suggestions: Overlock stitch, super-stretch stitch, double overlock stitch

Foot: . . . . Zigzag or embroidery foot
Stitch length: . . Stretch-stitch or cam setting
Stitch width: . . 4mm.

1. Test-sew on a fabric scrap to choose the stitch most compatible with your fabric.
2. Pin fabric pieces with right sides together.
3. Guide seam allowance so the needle bites into the fabric on the left and swings off the raw edge on the right. Pull pins out as you get to them.

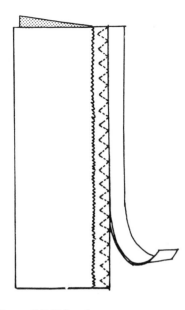

Figure 5-7 Trim the excess seam allowance and press.

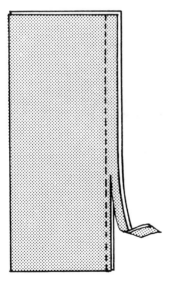

4. Trim excess seam allowance. Press finished seam allowance to one side.

SEAM FINISHES FOR LIGHTWEIGHT KNIT AND WOVEN FABRICS

Fine fabrics often create unusual sewing problems because the fabric curls, ravels, or is slippery to work with. The following seam treatments are recommended for lightweight knits such as nylon tricot, jersey, or Qiana, and lightweight woven fabrics such as gauze, batiste, voile, and crepe de chine. The finished seam allowance is ¼-inch (6mm.).

Straight-Stitch Sewing Machine

The traditional seam finish for lightweight fabrics is the French seam. This two-step finish can be used on straight and slightly curved seams and is both seam and seam finish.

Stitch: . . . . Straight stitch
Foot: . . . . Straight-stitch foot
Stitch length: . . 1½ to 2mm. or fine setting

1. Pin seam with the *wrong* sides of fabric together.
2. Place fabric under the presser foot ⅜-inch (9mm.) from the raw edge and stitch the seam.
3. Trim seam to ⅛-inch (3mm.) and press seam open. Encase raw edges by folding seam *right* sides together so the stitched line is on the fold (figure 5-8).
4. Stitch seam a second time on the wrong side, ⅛-inch (3mm.) from finished edge.
5. Press finished seam to one side (figure 5-8).

Figure 5-8 French seam.

Zigzag Sewing Machine

Stitch Suggestions: Zigzag stitch or interlock stitch

Foot: . . . . Zigzag foot
Stitch length: . . ¾ to 1mm. or fine setting
Stitch width: . . 4mm.

Reverse-Action Sewing Machine

Stitch: . . . . Picot stitch
Foot: . . . . Zigzag foot
Stitch length: . . Stretch-stitch or cam setting
Stitch width: . . 2mm.

The following instructions are the same for both zigzag and reverse-action sewing machines—only the stitch differs.

1. Carefully pin the seam with right sides of fabric together.
2. Place fabric halfway under the presser foot so the needle bites into the fabric on the left and swings off the raw edge on the right (figure 5-9).
3. Stitch the seam, pulling pins out before getting to them. *Note:* The picot stitch, sewn by the reverse-action machine only, can be sewn on the ⅝-inch (15mm.) seamline, then the excess fabric trimmed away after stitching (figure 5-9).
4. Press finished seam to one side.

MATCHING STRIPES OR PLAIDS

Most solid-color fabrics are easier to sew because there is no definite pattern to match. Matching stripes or plaids takes a little more care in preparation and sewing. Seams do not have to be hand basted, and you do not have to lose your temper, to get a perfect match. The secret is in the pinning.

Straight-Stitch and Zigzag Sewing Machines

Stitch: . . . . Straight stitch
Foot: . . . . Straight-stitch or embroidery foot
Stitch length: . . 2 to 3mm. or 10 to 15 stitches per inch
Stitch width: . . 0mm.

1. Pin seam with right sides of fabric together, placing pins perpendicular to the stitching line.
2. Alternate each pin, so one is pinned from *east to west,* the next from *west to east.* Pin approximately every 2 inches (5cm.), matching the plaid or stripe.
3. Begin sewing slowly on the seamline, carefully pulling pins out *before* you get to them.

Figure 5-9 Interlock and picot-stitch seam finish.

Reverse-Action Sewing Machine

This technique is great for T-shirt knits, sweater knits, and swimsuit fabrics that have a tendency to *scoot* while sewing—that is, the top layer of fabric will slide ahead of the bottom layer even though they are pinned together. The stitch helps match plaids and stripes, and will stretch with knit garments. *Hint:* For cross-grain shoulder seams on knit fabrics, place a strand of elastic thread under the foot and stitch over it as you sew the seam. This prevents shoulder seams from drooping out of shape when the garment is on a hanger.

Stitch: .... Super-stretch stitch or overlock stitch
Foot: .... Zigzag or embroidery foot
Stitch length: .. Stretch-stitch or cam setting
Stitch width: .. 4mm.

1. Pin seam with right sides of fabric together, placing pins perpendicular to the stitching line.

2. Alternate each pin, so one is pinned from *east to west,* the next from *west to east.* Pin approximately every 2 inches (5cm.), matching the plaid or stripe.

3. Using the super-stretch stitch or the overlock stitch, begin sewing on the seamline, placing the fabric so the left side of the stitch will be on the seamline. *Note:* For ¼-inch (6mm.) seams, place fabric under the foot so the left side of stitch falls on the ¼-inch (6mm.) seamline. Remember to pull pins out *before* you get to them (figure 5-10). The forward-and-reverse-feeding action of the stitch feeds the plaid or stripe evenly for a perfect match. Trim seam up to the stitch where necessary.

Figure 5-10 Remove pins before stitching over them.

REINFORCING STRESS SEAMS (CROTCH, UNDERARM, AND POCKET SEAMS)

All too often, these seams are the first ones to tear, especially in children's clothes. You will save a lot of time mending if you reinforce these seams as you make the garment.

Straight-Stitch Sewing Machine

Stitch: . . . . Straight stitch
Foot: . . . . Straight-stitch foot
Stitch length: . . 1mm. or fine setting

Set your machine as described and sew two rows of stitching approximately ⅛-inch (3mm.) apart.

One row of stitching will be on the seamline, the other in the seam allowance. By using a very short stitch, there is more thread in the seam. This allows more *give* and, therefore, more durability (figure 5-11). *Note:* Make sure the garment fits before the final stitching, because this stitch is almost impossible to rip out.

Zigzag Sewing Machine

Stitch: . . . . Zigzag stitch
Foot: . . . . Zigzag or embroidery foot
Stitch length: . . 1mm. or fine setting
Stitch width: . . 1mm.

Sew one row of tiny zigzag stitches in stress seams, on the seamline. Because the stitch length is very short, and the zigzag width narrow, there is a lot of thread in the seam. This enables the seam to withstand a lot of abuse in work and play clothes (figure 5-12). *Note:* Make sure the garment fits before the final stitching, because this stitch is almost impossible to rip out.

Reverse-Action Sewing Machine

Stitch: . . . . Straight-stretch stitch
Foot: . . . . Zigzag or embroidery foot
Stitch length: . . Stretch-stitch or cam setting
Stitch width: . . 0mm.

After fitting the garment, sew one row of the straight-stretch stitch in the stress seams. This stitch has more give when used in stress areas than any other stitch, and enables the seam to return to its original shape. It is copied from the hand backstitch used in stress seams by tailors, and is made with two stitches feeding forward and one back (figure 5-13). *Note:* Make sure the garment fits before the final stitching, because this stitch is almost impossible to rip out.

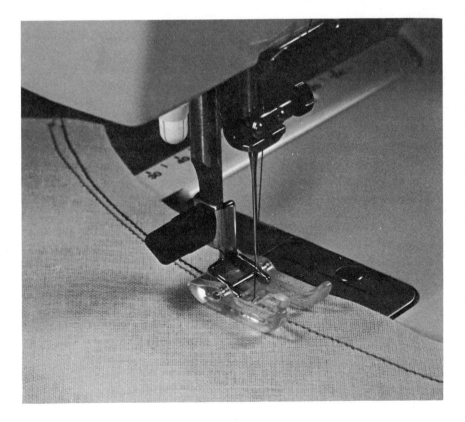

Figure 5-11 Reinforcing seams (straight-stitch machine).

Figure 5-12 Reinforcing seams (zigzag machine).

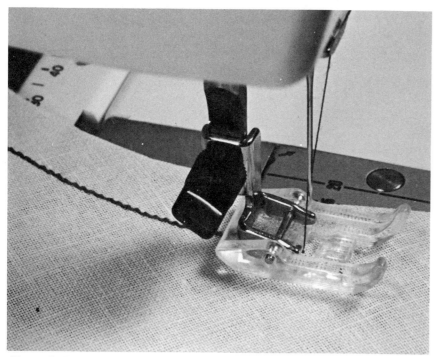

Figure 5-13 Reinforcing seams (reverse-action machine).

UNDERSTITCHING

Understitching is a common tailoring technique used around necklines, armholes, and under collars to keep facings from rolling to the right side of the garment. By understitching you can achieve more professional results and save time you would have spent on pressing.

Straight-Stitch Sewing Machine

Stitch: .... Straight stitch
Foot: .... Straight-stitch foot
Stitch length: .. 2 to 4mm. or 6 to 15 stitches per inch

Zigzag and Reverse-Action Sewing Machines

Stitch: .... Multiple-zigzag stitch
Foot: .... Zigzag or embroidery foot
Stitch length: .. 1½ to 2mm. or 15 to 20 stitches per inch
Stitch width: .. 4mm.

The procedure is the same for all machines:

1. After sewing facing on, clip through seam allowance almost up to the stitching line in the curved areas. *Do not clip through the stitches.*
2. Push the seam toward the facing and press.
3. With the right side up, place the facing under the foot so the seamline is about ¼-inch (6mm.) to the left of the needle.

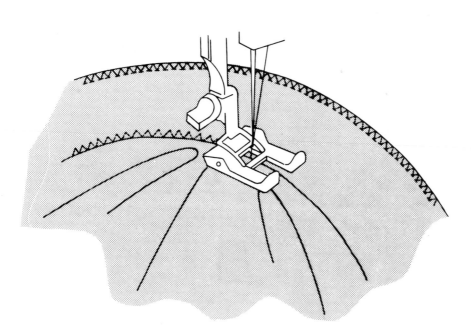

Figure 5-14 Understitching.

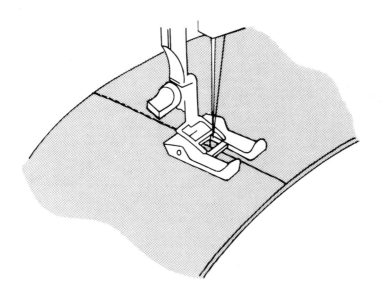

Figure 5-15 Stitching in the ditch.

4. Using a straight stitch or multiple-zigzag stitch, understitch close to the seamline on the facing side, catching the seam allowance underneath (figure 5-14). After the understitching is complete, trim excess seam allowance close to the understitching.

5. Press facing toward the inside of garment.

6. Tack facing to garment by hand or sew a few machine stitches through the facing in the shoulder seam, or in the underarm seam for armhole facings. This is called *stitching in the ditch*, because the stitches are sewn in the seamline and are hidden in the ditch or crack of the seam (figure 5-15).

TOPSTITCHING

Topstitching is one of the most common ways to give a home-made garment a tailored look. A topstitch can be sewn with a straight stitch using two threads or special topstitching thread (silk twist or polyester topstitching thread) through an American size 14, or European size 90, topstitching needle. A saddle-stitched effect can be created on the zigzag and reverse-action sewing machine as described on page 42, or by *couching* over pearl cotton or embroidery floss. To get that really professional topstitch, try one of the following methods.

Straight-Stitch Sewing Machine

Stitch: . . . . Straight stitch
Foot: . . . . Straight-stitch
foot
Stitch length: . . 4mm or 6
stitches per inch

For a defined topstitch on tailored garments, use the longest stitch length on medium to heavy fabrics. Use a slightly shorter stitch length on lighter-weight fabrics. In every case, use the same stitch length to topstitch all parts of the garment. When the collar is topstitched with a 2mm. stitch length, and the cuffs with a 4mm. stitch length, it is a dead

giveaway that the garment is homemade. As mentioned before, you can use two threads through a topstitching needle (figure 5-16). If a topstitching needle is not available in your area, an all-purpose American size 14, or European size 90, needle will work. Occasionally, when topstitching a pocket or collar, the machine will skip a stitch when pivoting at the corner. To prevent this, stop and pivot the work when the needle is on its way up, but not out of the fabric. The stitch cycle is not interrupted. This avoids skipped stitches.

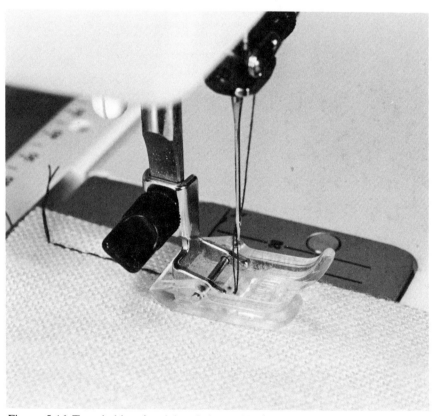

Figure 5-16 Topstitching (straight-stitch machine).

Zigzag Sewing Machine

Stitch: . . . . Blind-hem stitch
Foot: . . . . Cording and
braiding foot
Stitch length: . . 1 to 1 ½mm. or
fine setting
Stitch width: . . 2mm.

I love to see what manufacturers have done in ready-to-wear so I can get the same look in my own wardrobe. I remember how excited I was to learn that *London Fog* topstitched their $100 raincoats by couching over a piece of pearl-cotton cording or embroidery floss with a blind-hem stitch.

1. Thread the machine with the same color top and bobbin thread as the pearl cotton or floss that you will couch over.

2. Thread one or two strands of pearl cotton or floss through the cording and braiding foot, so the needle takes a few straight stitches next to the pearl cotton or floss on the right, and swings over it on the left in the blind-stitch formation. The straight stitches bury themselves into the fabric next to the pearl cotton or floss, and the small zigzag stitch makes an indentation over it to give the appearance of a long saddle stitch (figure 5-17).

3. To pivot the corner of a pocket or collar, let the needle swing over the pearl cotton or floss and back to the right side of the stitch. While needle is in the fabric, on its way up, pivot the work. This insures a square, crisp corner.

Figure 5-17 Blind-hem stitch couching over pearl cotton.

Reverse-Action Sewing Machine

Stitch: . . . . Couching stitch
Foot: . . . . Cording and braiding foot
Stitch length: . . Stretch-stitch or cam setting
Stitch width: . . 2mm.

1. Thread machine with same color top and bobbin thread as the pearl cotton or floss that you will couch over. *Hint:* Nylon monofilament thread works great for this technique because it is clear and blends with any color pearl cotton or fabric. To prevent thread from spilling off its spool and backlashing around the spool pin, put a plastic drinking straw over the spool pin. Then place the spool of thread over the straw. The straw hugs the inside of the spool, and the thread will not spill.

2. Thread one or two strands of floss into the cording and braiding foot and begin stitching. The straight stitches bury themselves in the fabric beside the pearl cotton or floss as the stitch swings over it and back. This combination gives the illusion of a long saddle stitch (figure 5-18).

3. To pivot at the corner of a pocket or collar, let the needle zigzag over the floss and back. While the needle is in the fabric, on its way up, pivot the work. This topstitch will appear professional to your most fashion-conscious friends.

Figure 5-18 Couching stitch over pearl cotton.

ZIPPER TRICKS

There are things about every craft or hobby that are routine and often dull. For me, it is zipper insertion, but with some help from cellophane or basting tape, the job can be a lot less tedious. The following technique is applicable to both centered and lapped zippers and can be sewn on all sewing machines with the use of a zipper foot.

1. Baste a ⅝-inch (15mm.) seam the length of the zipper using a long, straight stitch and a loosened upper tension. Without removing fabric from the machine, return upper tension to normal setting and shorten the stitch length for regular sewing. Finish sewing the seam. Press seam open. *Hint:* A loosened upper tension for basting will allow you to pull these stitches out easily.

2. Buy a zipper 1 inch (2.5cm.) longer than you need and place it face down in the seam allowance in the zipped position—on the inside of the seam. The zipper pull must be *up* on the extra length of the zipper tape (figure 5-19). *Note:* For a lapped zipper application, stitch right side of zipper as instructed on zipper package and press.

3. Instead of hand basting the zipper, tape zipper down with cellophane tape across the wrong side of the zipper about every 1- to 1½-inches (2.5 to 3.8cm.) (figure 5-19). Test the tape on your fabric first to make sure it will not damage it.

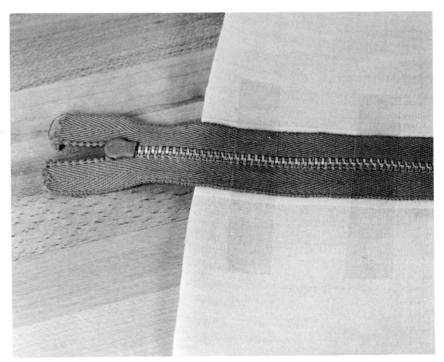

Figure 5-19 Zipper taped in place on wrong side before stitching.

Figure 5-20 Stitch zipper with tape template.

4. On the right side of fabric, place a strip of ½ inch (1.3cm.) wide tape the length of the zipper centering the seamline down the center of the tape for a *slot* or centered application. For lapped application, place the straight edge of the tape along the basted seamline.

5. Using the tape as a stitching guide, stitch the zipper in place from the *right* side of the garment, being careful *not* to stitch through the tape. This way, the stitching lines are parallel (figure 5-20).

6. Remove tape and basting stitches and pull the zipper pull down to the bottom of zipper.

7. Cut the extra length of zipper off the top. By hand, make thread tacks or place pins at the point where the zipper has been cut. (You would not want to accidently pull the zipper off the track.)

8. Stitch the waistband or facing in place immediately, catching the top of the zipper in the seam. The fabric will act as the zipper stop (figure 5-21).

This method is often used in men's pant construction. It saves a lot of time otherwise spent ripping out an irregular topstitch that bulges around the zipper pull.

Figure 5-21 Stitch waistband.

EASING IN A SLEEVE CAP

In my many home economics courses, I was required to make projects with set-in sleeves. To set in a sleeve, I used every pin in my pin cushion and often every nasty word in my vocabulary before I was able to hand baste the sleeve in place without puckers.

Have you ever had this experience, or avoided patterns with set-in sleeves for that reason? If so, the following technique will save you time and will not test your patience. The know-how is in your fingers, and it can be done on all types of fabric and with all types of sewing machines.

Stitch: . . . . Straight stitch
Foot: . . . . Straight-stitch or embroidery foot
Stitch length: . . 2 to 3mm. or 10 to 15 stitches per inch
Stitch width: . . 0mm.

1. Begin stitching at one of the notches in the sleeve cap, ½-inch (1.3cm.) from the raw edge. Using the index finger of your right and left hands simultaneously, pull fabric sideways exactly where the needle penetrates the fabric (figure 5-22).

2. Take four or five stitches, then reposition your fingers, pulling the fabric away from the needle, as described, until easing stitches have been sewn from notch to notch (figure 5-23). If more ease is desired, pull the fabric harder from side to side. The sleeve cap will have an *eased,* rather than pleated or gathered appearance.

Figure 5-22 Easing in sleeve cap.

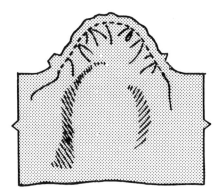

Figure 5-23 Eased sleeve cap.

3. Sew underarm sleeve seam and finish lower sleeve edge. Pin sleeve in place. If there is too much ease in the cap, clip a thread where necessary to flatten the work.

4. Place the eased side of the sleeve cap down against the feed dog on your machine and stitch along the seamline. Pull pins out as you go. You will find the action of the feed dog feeds the eased cap into the garment without puckers or homemade-looking pleats.

INVISIBLE POCKET APPLICATION

This invisible pocket application is suitable for unlined pockets with round corners and can be used on breast-sized to jacket-sized pockets. The pocket is stitched from the inside and can only be done on zigzag and reverse-action sewing machines.

1. Finish the top raw edge of pocket, fold a hem on pocket top, and press. *Stay stitch plus* around the curved pocket edges (see *Stay Stitching Plus,* page 64) (figure 5-24).

2. Press the pocket seam allowances to the inside.

3. Pin pocket in place and set your machine as follows:

Stitch: . . . . Zigzag stitch
Foot: . . . . Zigzag or
                      embroidery foot
Stitch length: . . 4mm. or 6
                   stitches per inch
Stitch width: . . 4mm.

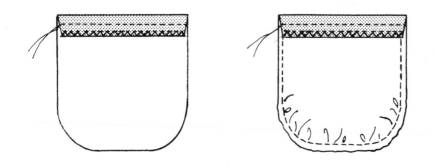

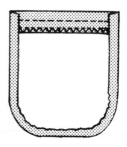

Figure 5-24 To make a pocket, ease, and press.

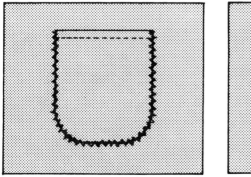

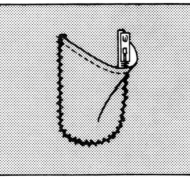

Figure 5-25 Zigzag baste, stitch pocket to garment.

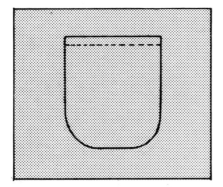

Figure 5-26 Finished pocket.

Loosen upper thread tension slightly.

4. Baste pocket, guiding the work so presser foot is half on the pocket and half on the body of the garment. *Note:* The needle will swing onto the pocket with one stitch and into the garment fabric with the next (figure 5-25).

5. Reset upper tension to normal setting. Reset machine as follows:

Stitch: . . . . Straight or zigzag stitch
Foot: . . . . Zigzag or embroidery foot
Stitch length: . . 2mm. or 15 stitches per inch
Stitch width: . . 01mm.

6. Reach into the pocket and spread open the seam allowance as pictured at right in figure 5-25. The zigzag basting stitches look like ladder rungs across the seamline.

7. Using the tiny zigzag stitch described, stitch inside the pocket in the seamline along the pressed fold. Complete stitching around entire inside pocket seam.

8. Pull basting stitches out and the pocket will stay in place almost forever (figure 5-26).

ELASTIC APPLICATION

Have you ever carefully sewn a piece of elastic into a project just to find that your masterpiece fits comfortably around your hips instead of your waistline? If so, the reason is that you probably stretched the elastic when you sewed it, and broke down the rubber knitted or woven into the elastic. The following techniques teach you how to sew elastic into most anything without ruining the elastic in the process.

Measure the elastic comfortably around your waist, or wherever you intend to put it, and add ½-inch (1.3cm.) for overlap. *Note:* If this is going into a waistband on a pair of pants, be sure the elastic will stretch over your hips.

Elastic Casing at an Edge

This is an easy alternative to tunnel casing. With this method, you can insure that the elastic will not twist when the garment is worn.

Straight-Stitch Sewing Machine

Stitch: . . . . Straight stitch
Foot: . . . . Straight-stitch
 foot
Stitch length: . . 2mm. or 15
 stitches per inch

Zigzag Sewing Machine

Stitch: . . . . Zigzag stitch
Foot: . . . . Zigzag or
 embroidery foot
Stitch length: . . 1mm. or fine
 setting
Stitch width: . . 1mm.

Reverse-Action Sewing Machine

Stitch: . . . . Super-stretch
 stitch
Foot: . . . . Zigzag or
 embroidery foot
Stitch length: . . Stretch-stitch or
 cam setting
Stitch width: . . 4mm.

1. Lap and seam elastic ends. Mark elastic off into four equal parts, marking with pins.

2. Finish raw edge of fabric, (woven fabrics only) then fold waistline edge to the inside of garment to make a casing the width of the elastic plus ½-inch (1.3cm.), and press.

3. Pin elastic into the waistline with elastic edge up into the folded casing. Match pins on elastic with center front, center back, and side seams.

4. Stitch casing down. Stretch elastic as you sew to keep the fabric flat and the stitches *below* the elastic (figure 5-27). If you stitch through it, the elastic will break down and stretch out of shape. Trim excess fabric for knits only. This method is much faster than trying to thread a strip of elastic through a casing.

5. *Stitch in the ditch,* (page 54) at center front, center back, and the two side seams through elastic and casing so elastic will not turn in casing.

Figure 5-27 Elastic sewn into a casing.

Elastic Stitched in Casing at an Edge

This method is set up for zig-zag and reverse-action sewing machines. It works well in knit fabrics, from stretch terry to swimwear, and prevents elastic from twisting in the casing. *Note:* You will have to allow at least ½-inch (1.3cm.) more fabric at the top opening when cutting the garment out.

Zigzag and Reverse-Action Sewing Machines: Easing Fabric into Elastic

Stitch: .... Multiple-zigzag stitch
Foot: .... Zigzag or embroidery foot
Stitch length:.. 1mm. or fine setting
Stitch width: .. 4mm.

1. Divide elastic into four equal parts, marking each part with a pin. Do not join ends. Divide waistline opening into four equal parts, marking each part with a pin.

2. Pin elastic into waistline matching pins *½-inch (1.3cm.) down from the raw edge on the wrong side of the garment.*

3. Place work under the presser foot and sew a couple of stitches to anchor elastic. Using the index fingers of the right and left hands simultaneously, begin sewing and pull fabric out sideways exactly where the needle penetrates the fabric. As you pull out with your fingers, push the fabric slightly under the needle as well, to ease in the fabric.

4. Take four or five stitches,

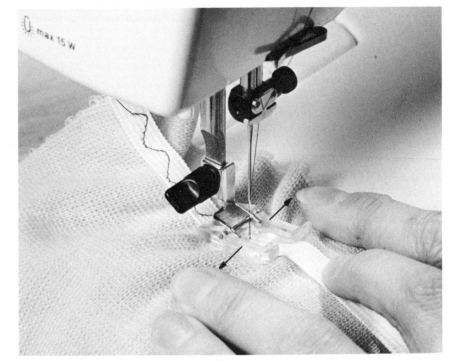

Figure 5-28 Elastic application (step 1).

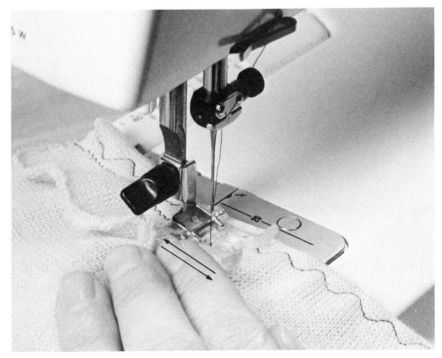

Figure 5-29 Elastic application (step 2).

then reposition your fingers, pulling the fabric away from the needle at the sides as described previously until the elastic has been eased into the garment (figure 5-28). If more ease is needed, pull the fabric out more firmly from side to side. Overlap elastic ends when you have completed stitching all the way around the garment.

Zigzag Sewing Machine: Final stitching of elastic in casing

Stitch: . . . . Zigzag, interlock, or multistretch stitch
Foot: . . . . Zigzag foot
Stitch length: . . 1½ to 2mm. or 15 to 20 stitches per inch
Stitch width: . . 1mm.

Reverse-Action Sewing Machine

Stitch: . . . . Super-stretch or double overlock stitch
Foot: . . . . Zigzag or embroidery foot
Stitch length: . . Stretch-stitch or cam setting
Stitch width: . . 4mm.

1. Fold fabric down so the elastic is encased in the fabric, and the stitching is seen on the wrong side of the work.
2. On the wrong side, place the left index finger to the left side of the foot and sew under elastic while moving the fabric back and forth. This trick prevents the elastic from stretching out of shape and eliminates unnecessary puckers, tucks, or gathers from being stitched into the right side of the work (figure 5-29).
3. Use a pair of sharp scissors to trim the excess fabric from the raw edge of the casing.

Lingerie Elastic Application

The following one-step technique is recommended for lingerie. It is only for zigzag and reverse-action machines.

Zigzag Sewing Machine

Stitch Suggestions: Multistretch stitch or multiple-zigzag stitch

Foot: . . . . Zigzag or embroidery foot
Stitch length: . . 1mm. or fine setting
Stitch width: . . 4mm. for ½-inch (1.3cm.) elastic; 2mm. for ¼-inch (6mm.) elastic.

Reverse-Action Sewing Machine

Stitch: . . . . Overlock stitch
Foot: . . . . Zigzag or embroidery foot
Stitch length: . . Stretch-stitch or cam setting
Stitch width: . . 4mm. for ½-inch (1.3cm.) elastic; 2mm. for ¼-inch (6mm.) elastic

1. Cut lingerie with ½-inch (1.3cm.) extra fabric at the top of waistline for half-slips and panties, and at panty legs where elastic is to be sewn.
2. Measure elastic to fit comfortably around the waist and/or legs (usually 2 to 5 inches [5 to 12.5cm.] smaller than garment-opening measurement), and divide elastic into four or eight equal parts. Mark each part with a pin.

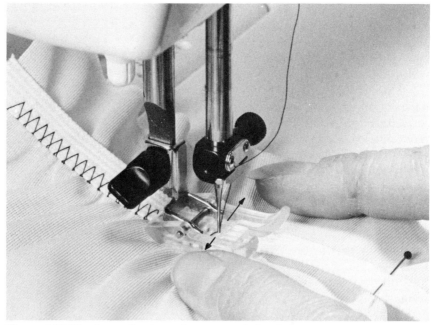

Figure 5-30 Elastic application using an overlock stitch.

3. Match pins on elastic with pins on waistline, placing elastic ½-inch (1.3cm.) down from the opening on the right side of the garment. Overlap and pin elastic ends at side seam. *Note:* Lingerie elastic should always be sewn on the outside of the garment, away from the body, so body oils and perspiration do not damage elastic.

4. For panties, pin elastic on leg openings, leaving side seams open. After elastic is sewn, stitch side seams through elastic ends.

5. Place work under presser foot so the left side of the stitch falls on the tricot and the right side of the stitch swings onto elastic.

6. Begin sewing. Using index fingers of both hands simultaneously, pull fabric out sideways exactly where the needle penetrates elastic (figure 5-30). Sew a few stitches, then reposition your fingers, pulling the fabric away from the needle while pushing the fabric slightly to ease it into place. *Note:* If more ease is desired, pull fabric more firmly from side to side. For less ease, do not pull fabric as hard. Do not shove fabric into elastic. This creates uncomfortable gathers around elasticized areas. *Hint:* For more practice in the technique, see page 58 for setting in sleeves. The hand posture is the same in both cases.

7. After tricot has been eased into the elastic, secure elastic ends and trim excess fabric up to the stitching line. Then sew a ribbon or bow where elastic ends overlap.

HEMS

Your sewing machine can be your best friend when it's time for sewing a hem. Many different hems are explained here that can be used as decorative touches. First, however, is a machine method that can eliminate hand hemming.

Easing in a Hemline on a Flared Skirt

With the fashion trend going back to more feminine dressing, many of us are faced with the problem of hemming flared, bias-cut, wrap, or other skirts with curved hemlines. This easy method, called *stay stitching plus,* saves time and can even be used on a full circle skirt with any type of sewing machine.

Hang the finished garment overnight before marking and hemming. The fabric relaxes, and the weight of the garment pulls on the seams and any bias-cut sections. An even hem can then be measured and sewn.

Stitch: . . . . Straight stitch
Foot: . . . . Straight or embroidery foot
Stitch length:.. 2 to 3mm. or 10 to 15 stitches per inch
Stitch width: .. 0mm.

1. Overcast the raw hem edge with the zigzag, multiple-zigzag, or overlock stitch (pages 15 and 17), or pink the edge.

2. Place finished hemline under the presser foot with the needle ¼-inch (6mm.) from the finished edge.

3. Hold the fabric firmly behind the presser foot and begin sewing. The fabric should pile up behind the foot. Continue sewing and hold the fabric firmly until you cannot hold the piled-up fabric any longer (figure 5-31).

4. Repeat the process until the easing stitches have been sewn around the hemline.

5. Fold up hem to the desired amount, and steam press folded edge, using a press cloth (figure 5-32). Do not press directly on the eased area.

6. Finish the hem with a hand or machine blind stitch as follows.

Blind-Hemming by Machine

Inevitably, it seems, a hem must be put up at the last minute—before school or work—and who has the half hour or forty-five minutes in the morning to put up a hem by hand? Once you have mastered machine blind-hemming, I doubt you will put another hem in by hand. This method is for zigzag and reverse-action machines, and is great for both straight and curved hems that have been eased into place as described in the previous section.

Stitch: . . . . Blind-hem or stretch-blind-hem stitch (for knits)
Foot: . . . . Blind-hem foot
Stitch length:.. 2 to 3mm. or 10 to 15 stitches per inch
Stitch width: .. 2mm.

1. Measure hem. On a woven fabric, finish raw edge with the

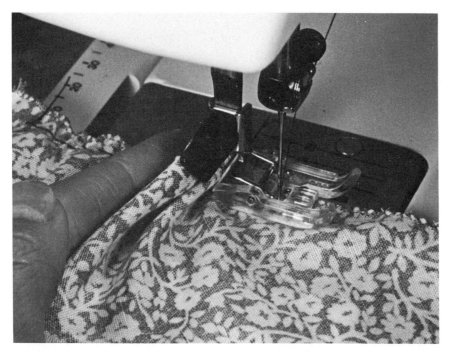

Figure 5-31 Easing in hemline.

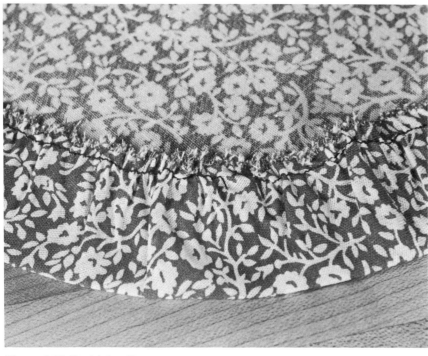

Figure 5-32 Eased hemline.

multiple-zigzag stitch or overlock stitch explained on pages 15 and 17.

2. Fold the hem up to the desired amount and press. *Hint:* You may want to baste the hem in place ½-inch (1.3cm.) up from the folded edge, but it is not necessary.

3. Fold the hem to the outside of the garment. Place this fold under the presser foot with the body of the garment to the left and at least ¼-inch (6mm.) of the hem fabric to the right of the needle. The wing of the blind-hem foot should be against the fold.

4. Begin sewing. The needle will take a few stitches on the ¼-inch (6mm.) hem extension, then bite into the fold (figure 5-33). Be sure the needle only picks up a thread or two of the fabric when it swings into the fold. *Hint:* For a truly invisible blind hem, loosen the upper and lower tension and use a very fine needle and thread.

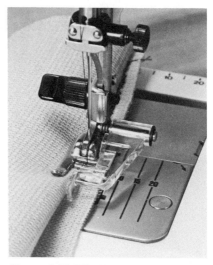

Figure 5-33 Blind-hemming.

T-shirt and Sweater Hems

Many home sewers avoid making T-shirts and/or sweaters because, no matter what hemming technique is used, stitches often break after the garment has been worn a few times. The following method is quick, easy, and will help eliminate that problem. It can be used with any model sewing machine and makes the hem look like it has been knitted into the garment. The secret is the elastic thread that stretches and keeps the hem in shape.

Stitch: . . . . Straight stitch
Foot: . . . . Straight-stitch
                 foot
Stitch length: . . 3mm. or 10
                 stitches per inch.
Stitch width: . . 0mm.

1. Thread bobbin with elastic thread and loosen the bobbin tension so there is little or no drag on the bobbin thread. If your machine has a bobbin case with a tension by-pass hole, thread the elastic thread through the hole as illustrated on page 108.

2. Press hem up to the desired amount. Place fabric under the presser foot, right side up. Be sure the presser foot is resting on a double layer of fabric (figure 5-34).

3. Topstitch the hem in place. Do not backstitch. Tie off elastic thread ends securely by hand.

4. Carefully trim the excess fabric away from the hem up to the stitching line.

Twin-Needle Hem

Twin-needle hemming works beautifully on both knit and woven fabrics and adds a decorative touch as well. Top and bobbin should be threaded with the same color thread as the fashion fabric.

Zigzag Sewing Machine (top- or front-loading bobbin machines only)

Stitch: . . . . Straight stitch
Foot: . . . . Embroidery foot
Stitch length: . . 2 to 3mm. or 10
                 to 15 stitches per
                 inch
Stitch width: . . 0mm.

For a flatter hem finish, loosen upper tension slightly.

1. Press hem up to the desired amount and pin. Place fabric under the presser foot, right side up, with the fold even with the edge of the presser foot. Be sure the foot is resting on a double layer of fabric.

2. Topstitch hem in place, using the edge of the presser foot as a guide. Remove pins as you sew (figure 5-35).

3. Press hem. Carefully trim the excess hem allowance from the wrong side of the garment up to the stitching line.

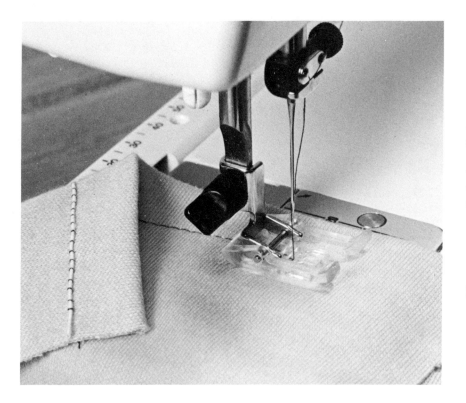

Figure 5-34 Elastic-thread hem.

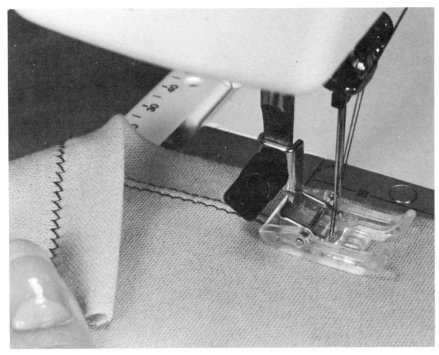

Figure 5-35 Twin-needle hem.

Topstitched Hem

This professional-looking hem finish is often used by ready-to-wear manufacturers to give the inside-out look to T-shirts and jeans.

Reverse-Action Sewing Machine

Stitch Suggestions: Overlock or double overlock stitch

Foot: . . . . Embroidery foot
Stitch length: . . Stretch-stitch or cam setting
Stitch width: . . 4mm.

1. Test for desired stitch on fabric scrap.
2. Press hem up to the desired amount and pin in place. Place fabric under the presser foot, right side up. Be sure foot is resting on a double layer of fabric.
3. Topstitch hem in place, removing pins as you sew (figure 5-36).
4. Trim the excess fabric away from the hem allowance up to stitching line.

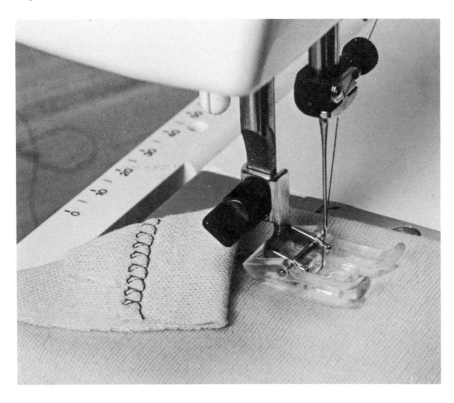

Figure 5-36 Double-overlock hem.

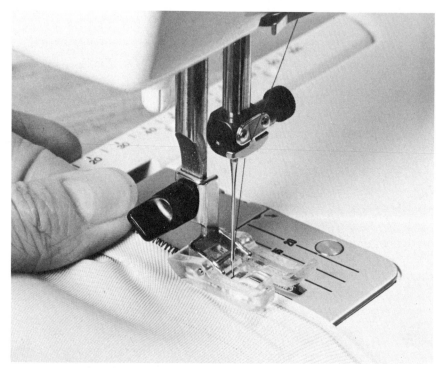

Figure 5-37 Lettuce hem (method 1).

Lettuce Hem

For a feminine hem or edge finish on lightweight knit fabrics such as nylon tricot, jersey, and interlock knits, try the lettuce hem. It is done with a zigzag or reverse-action machine only.

Stitch: . . . . Zigzag stitch
Foot: . . . . Embroidery or zigzag foot
Stitch length: . . ½ to ¾mm. or fine setting
Stitch width: . . 4mm.

Method 1

This technique only applies to single knits such as nylon tricot, because this fabric curls automatically to the right side when stretched on the cross grain.

1. Stretch raw hem edge on the cross grain. The fabric will roll to the right side.
2. Place rolled hem edge under the left groove in the embroidery foot, supporting the fabric in front and behind the presser foot with your hands (figure 5-37).
3. Stitch lettuce hem by letting the needle catch the rolled edge on the left and swing off the edge at the right, gently stretching fabric as you go. This hem finish is ideal for nightgown hems.

Figure 5-38 Lettuce hem (method 2).

Method 2

For stretchier fabrics and those that can run, such as hosiery, T-shirt ribbing, and interlock knits, sew the lettuce hem like this:

1. Turn the hem edge under ½-inch (1.3cm.).

2. Place folded hem edge halfway under the zigzag foot so the needle catches the fabric on the left and swings off folded edge at the right. Stitch the edge *without* stretching the fabric. The stitches are so close together that they automatically push the fabric out of shape, thus creating the lettuce hem (figure 5-38).

3. Trim excess fabric up to the stitching line. *Note:* For a heavier edge, stitch over the lettuce hem a second time with a slightly longer zigzag stitch.

4. After trimming, stretch the hem on the cross grain for a curlier edge.

Shell-Tuck Hem

This attractive stitching technique is commonly found on lingerie, evening wear, and children's clothing. It can be used on both knit and woven fabrics.

Zigzag Sewing Machine

Stitch: . . . . Blind- or stretch-blind-hem stitch
Foot: . . . . Embroidery or zigzag foot
Stitch length: . . 1½ to 2mm. or 15 to 20 stitches per inch
Stitch width: . . 4mm.

1. Turn up hem, press, and pin in place.

2. Feed right side of folded hem edge under the presser foot, from the *right,* so the needle bites into the fabric on the right and swings off folded edge on the left. Be sure the needle swings completely off fabric edge at the left to avoid skipped stitches. Remove pins as you sew.

3. For a special decorative treatment, place a piece of pearl cotton or embroidery floss under the left side of the foot, and let the needle couch over it (figure 5-39).

4. Sew a row of decorative stitching above shell tuck as described on page 69, or trim excess fabric away up to the stitching line.

Reverse-Action Sewing Machine

Stitch: . . . . Couching stitch
Foot: . . . . Zigzag foot
Stitch length: . . Stretch-stitch or cam setting
Stitch width: . . 4mm.

Note: This method of shell-hemming is done with the bulk of the fabric to the *left,* and is easier than the previous technique when working with a slip or nightgown.

1. Fold hem up at least 1 inch (2.5cm.) and press. Pin in place.

2. Place folded hem edge halfway under the presser foot so the needle bites into fabric on the *left* and swings off folded edge at the right. Remove pins as you sew. Needle must swing com-

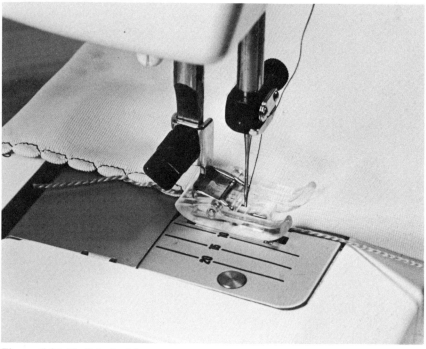

Figure 5-39 Shell-tucked hem.

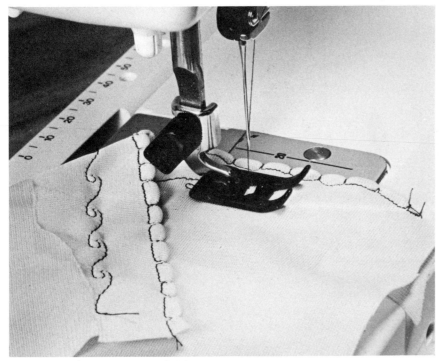

Figure 5-40 Decorative hem finish.

pletely off the folded edge to avoid skipped stitches.

Before trimming excess fabric away from the shell-tucked edge, you might like to sew one or more rows of decorative stitching above the shell tuck on the doubled hem (figure 5-40). The following stitches work well:

Zigzag Sewing Machine

Stitch Suggestions: Scallop stitch, multiple-zigzag stitch

Foot: . . . . Zigzag foot
Stitch length: . . 1½ to 2mm. or 15 to 20 stitches per inch
Stitch width: . . 4mm.

Reverse-Action Sewing Machine

Stitch Suggestions: Wave stitch, Greek key, running daisy stitch

Foot: . . . . Zigzag foot
Stitch length: . . Stretch-stitch or cam setting
Stitch width: . . 4mm.

After decorative stitching is complete, trim excess fabric up to the stitching line or sew lace to the hemline as follows.

Figure 5-41 Lace hem treatment.

Lace Hemline Treatment

Have you ever walked behind someone and the wide lace hem on their lingerie was seen through their sheer skirt? The following lace hem treatment eliminates this problem and prevents the lace from snagging your pantyhose because it is applied over the tricot hem.

Straight-Stitch Sewing Machine

Stitch: . . . . Straight stitch
Foot: . . . . Straight-stitch foot
Stitch length: . . 1 to 1½mm. or fine setting to 20 stitches per inch

Zigzag Sewing Machine

Stitch: . . . . Zigzag stitch
Foot: . . . . Zigzag or embroidery foot
Stitch length: . . 1 to 1½mm. or fine setting to 20 stitches per inch
Stitch width: . . 1mm.

Reverse-Action Sewing Machine

Stitch: . . . . Picot stitch
Foot: . . . . Zigzag or embroidery foot
Stitch length: . . . Stretch-stitch or cam setting
Stitch width: . . 2mm.

1. Measure around the hem and cut lace the length of hemline plus 1 inch (2.5cm.). Seam lace as described on page 107, and tie off thread ends securely.
2. Turn up hem on the right side of garment the width of lace plus ½-inch (1.3cm.). Press. Shell-tuck folded edge (page 69) if desired.
3. Pin lace around hemline on the right side of the garment, so the bottom of lace is even with the folded or machine-finished edge. Be sure that the top of lace is on a double layer of fabric.
4. Stitch lace on hemline, about ⅛-inch (3mm.) from its top edge (figure 5-41).
5. Carefully trim excess fabric above stitching line.

Chapter 6

BUTTONHOLES MADE EASY

Have you ever looked through the pattern catalogs and avoided choosing a pattern because it called for buttonholes? The following pages will give you the confidence to tackle any pattern—no matter how many buttonholes are required.

Even though buttonholers are not built into straight-stitch sewing machines, buttonholes can be made easily and professionally with a buttonhole attachment. Buttonhole attachments are also available for zigzag and reverse-action machines if you are not able to master the built-in buttonholer. To insure that you buy the proper attachment, remember to tell your local dealer the approximate age, make, and model number of your machine.

BUTTONHOLE PLACEMENT FOR BUTTONHOLE ATTACHMENTS

Horizontal Buttonholes

1. Place a long strip of ½-inch (1.3 cm.) cellophane tape so one edge of the tape is along the center-front line of the finished closure. Test the tape on your fabric first to make sure it will not harm it.

2. For proper spacing, place shorter pieces of tape perpendicular to the first pieces, where the buttonholes are to be made (figure 6-1).

3. Buttonholes are made *next* to the tape because the needle may become gummy if it stitches through the tape, causing skipped stitches.

Vertical Buttonholes

1. Mark the top of the buttonhole with one strip of tape horizontal to closure. Test the tape on your fabric first to make sure it will not harm it.

2. Center the buttonhole by placing a second piece of tape perpendicular to the first.

3. Make buttonhole next to the vertical strip of tape, so buttonholes are on the straight of the grain (figure 6-2).

BUTTONHOLE PLACEMENT FOR BUILT-IN BUTTONHOLERS

Horizontal Buttonhole

1. Place a strip of ½-inch (1.3 cm.) cellophane tape along the center-front line of the finished closure with one edge of the tape on the center-front line. Test the

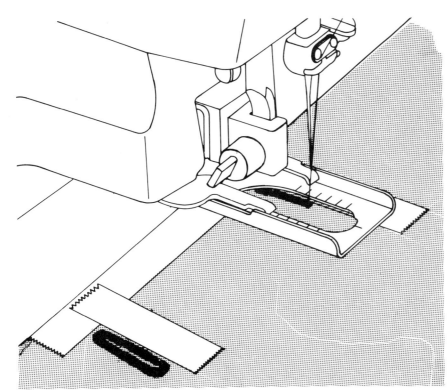

Figure 6-1 Horizontal buttonhole placement using attachment.

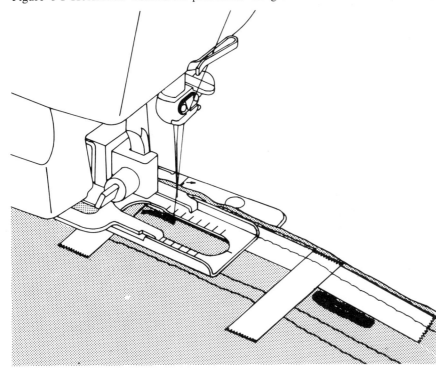

Figure 6-2 Vertical buttonhole.

tape on your fabric first to make sure it will not harm it.

2. For proper spacing, place shorter piece of tape perpendicular to the first piece where the top of the buttonhole will be (figure 6-3).

3. Measure the buttonhole length and place a third piece of tape parallel to the first. *Hint:* For proper buttonhole length, measure the diameter plus the depth of the button, then add an extra ⅛-inch (3mm.) for buttonhole bartacks.

4. Sew buttonholes from one piece of tape to the other, making bartacks when the needle gets close to the tape (figure 6-3).

Vertical Buttonhole

1. Place two horizontal strips of tape parallel to each other. The distance between tape is the desired length of the buttonhole, which is the diameter plus depth of button plus ⅛-inch (3mm.) for bartacks. Test the tape on your fabric first to make sure it will not harm it.

2. Place a third vertical strip of tape next to the center-front line to center the buttonhole on the straight of the grain.

3. Sew buttonholes from one piece of tape to the other, stitching *next* to the third piece of tape. When the needle gets close to the tape, make the bartacks and finish the buttonhole (figure 6-4).

Note: A buttonhole foot with a guide, to be used on zigzag and reverse-action machines, has been

Figure 6-3 Horizontal automatic buttonhole placement (step 4).

Figure 6-4 Vertical automatic buttonhole placement.

introduced to the home-sewing market. This foot will enable you to make all buttonholes of uniform size. The foot uses the actual button to determine buttonhole size. Mark buttonholes as described on page 72. This type of buttonhole foot is available for both low- and high-shank sewing machines and costs only a couple of dollars. To use it:

1. Place the button on the foot and push the small black bracket up to the edge of the button (see figure 2-11, page 21). Tighten screw.

2. Remove button. The foot slides the length needed for the buttonhole, including room for bartacks.

3. Put the foot on machine and make a manual or automatic buttonhole as follows (figure 6-5).

SEWING BUTTONHOLES WITH AN ATTACHMENT

After your buttonholes are accurately marked, stitching them is easy. If you are not sure how the buttonholes will look, practice stitching a few on scraps of your fabric.

Straight-Stitch Sewing Machine

Stitch: . . . . Straight stitch
Foot: . . . . Buttonhole attachment
Stitch length: . . Omm., Drop feed dog, or cover feed dog with darning plate

1. Insert proper template into attachment for buttonhole length. Turn knob on top of attachment so buttonhole starts at the beginning of the cycle.

2. Place attachment on the machine, making sure the fork is on the needle clamp and the attachment is securely screwed onto the presser bar.

3. Make a test buttonhole on same fabric thicknesses as finished garment. Cut buttonhole open to check that it will fit your button.

4. Place garment under attachment so the beginning of the buttonhole starts at the edge of the tape (figure 6-1, 6-2).

5. Step on the gas or press the knee control on your machine and the buttonhole is made in no time.

6. Remove tape after buttonholes are complete. Cut buttonholes open with a seam ripper or buttonhole scissors.

Keyhole Buttonholes

Keyhole buttonholes are most frequently found on ready-to-wear suits and coats. To make keyhole buttonholes that don't look homemade, use the buttonhole attachment. Most attachments come with keyhole templates. If you need extra templates for different sized buttons, buy them through your local sewing machine dealer.

This method is much easier than guessing at the buttonhole size and shape, or trying to find a tailor in town who will make them for you.

1. Make the keyhole buttonhole like any other buttonhole made with an attachment, as described on page 75.

2. Cut buttonhole open with a seam ripper or buttonhole scissor. Trim excess fabric close to the stitches.

3. Finish keyhole buttonhole by hand. Using buttonhole twist or topstitching thread, sew the hand buttonhole stitch over the machine stitches (figure 6-6).

Zigzag Sewing Machine

Manual Buttonhole

A manual buttonhole is so named because the buttonhole has to be made by turning the fabric to make the different sides of the buttonhole and by manipulating the stitch-width control.

Figure 6-6 Handworked keyhole buttonholes (step 3).

Figure 6-5 Placement of buttonhole foot with guide.

This buttonhole can be made on any sewing machine with a zigzag stitch but is only recommended for machines that *do not* have a built-in buttonholer.

Stitch: .... Zigzag stitch
Foot: .... Buttonhole foot
                or buttonhole
                foot with guide
Stitch length: .. ½mm. or fine
                setting
Stitch width: .. 2 to 4mm.

Left Needle Position

1. Set stitch width on 2mm and sew down the left side of the buttonhole, stopping with the needle in the right side of the stitch.

2. Lift presser foot and pivot the fabric 180°.

3. Lower presser foot and take the needle out of the work.

4. Move the stitch width to 4mm.

5. Holding the fabric firmly so it will not move, bartack the end of the buttonhole, letting the needle take a few stitches side to side. Return stitch width to 2mm.

6. Sew the second side of the buttonhole, stopping with the needle out of the fabric. Move the stitch width back to 4mm., and bartack as before.

7. Move stitch width to 0mm. and make a few straight stitches to lock off the buttonhole (figure 6-7). This eliminates tying threads off by hand.

Automatic Buttonhole

An automatic buttonhole can be made automatically on reverse-action and some zigzag machines without manually turning the fabric. Each brand has its patented process of making an automatic buttonhole. Specific instructions should be well illustrated in your sewing machine instruction book. The most common automatic buttonhole is made in four steps, where a dial or lever is used to make the two sides of the buttonhole and two bartacks. Buttonholes can be made the same size by using the buttonhole foot with guide (page 21) or one of the marking techniques described on page 72.

Corded Buttonholes

A corded buttonhole can be used in almost any garment, but is most commonly used on work clothes, coats, and suits that require a more rugged buttonhole. A corded buttonhole looks better than an ordinary buttonhole because it has a raised, denser appearance.

Stitch: .... Zigzag stitch
Foot: .... Buttonhole foot
Stitch length: .. ½mm. or fine
                setting
Stitch width: .. Automatic
                buttonhole
                setting

1. Use a piece of pearl cotton or embroidery floss the same color as the top and bobbin threads (waxed dental floss works well for white buttonholes).

2. Place cording under the buttonhole foot, being sure the loop of the cord will be at the stress point of the buttonhole. Always use a piece of cording a little longer than you need. *Hint:* Some buttonhole feet have prongs or grooves to easily anchor and hold the cord in place while sewing.

3. Make a manual or automatic buttonhole as previously described, making sure that the zigzag stitches cover the cord.

4. With the free ends, pull the loop of the cording to the bartack. Then pull cording ends through to the wrong side of the garment with a knit fixer, needle threader, or large-eyed needle and tie them off (figure 6-8). Cording ends should not be visible from the right side of the garment. The corded buttonhole lasts the life of the garment.

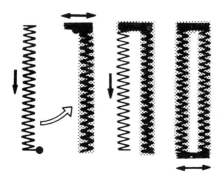

Figure 6-7 Manual buttonhole.

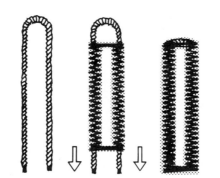

Figure 6-8 Corded buttonhole.

Easy Bound Buttonholes

I remember some of my teachers saying that bound buttonholes—buttonholes with fabric openings instead of stitched thread openings—added $5.00 per buttonhole to the value of the finished garment. I agreed with them, but I did not think it was worth $5.00 an hour to sew them properly until I learned this easy method for zigzag and reverse-action machines.

Stitch: . . . . Zigzag stitch
Foot: . . . . Buttonhole foot
Stitch length: . . ¾mm. or fine setting
Stitch width: . . 2mm. or automatic buttonhole setting

1. Mark buttonhole placement. Cut a piece of fashion fabric ¾-inch (18mm.) longer than the diameter of the button and 2-inches (5cm.) wide. Place this piece of fabric on the garment with right sides together where the buttonhole will be made. This buttonhole facing will be the lips of the bound buttonhole (figure 6-9A).

Make a buttonhole the proper length, either manually or with the built-in buttonholer on your machine, *omitting* the bartacks at either end of the buttonhole (figure 6-9B).

2. Using a short, straight stitch, approximately 1mm. or 20 stitches per inch, stitch a box around the outside of the buttonhole as close to the zigzag stitches as possible (figure 6-10A).

3. Cut the buttonhole open down the center, trimming excess fabric from between the two rows of stitching. Before getting to either end of the buttonhole, make angled clips to the straight-stitched corners of the box, forming a little triangle. Do not worry about cutting through the zigzag stitches at the end of the buttonhole (figure 6-10B).

4. Turn the buttonhole facing through the buttonhole (figure 6-11A). To form the lips, fold

Figures 6-9, 6-10, 6-11, 6-12 Steps in preparing an easy bound buttonhole.

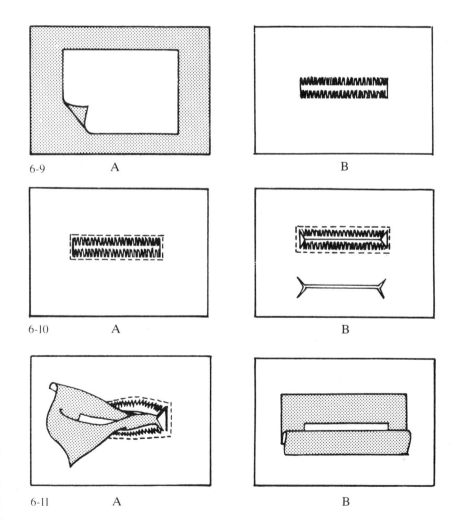

6-9   A   B

6-10   A   B

6-11   A   B

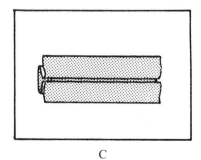

C

fabric back over the zigzagged buttonhole sides made in Step 1. This insures that both lips of the buttonhole are the same width (figure 6-11B & C).

5. Press fabric lips toward the center of the buttonhole. Sew a few locking stitches at both ends to square up the buttonhole (figure 6-12A).

6. Finish buttonhole by stitching in the ditch (page 54) on the right side of the buttonhole. Trim excess fabric from the wrong side of the fabric, leaving enough fabric so the lips will not ravel up to the stitching (figure 6-12B).

7. To finish front facing under bound buttonhole, cut a slit in it the length of, and in, the buttonhole. Turn raw edges under the slipstitch by hand around the buttonhole. *Note:* On lighter-weight fabrics, the facing can be finished as described in Steps 1 through 4. Then press the box shape so the lips of the buttonhole are pressed to the *outside* of the box, which is the inside of the facing. Hand stitch facing to the wrong side of bound buttonhole.

Reverse-Action Sewing Machine

Stretch Buttonhole

One of the trouble spots when sewing knit fabrics is making buttonholes. Buttonholes do not stay buttoned and often develop a fishmouth look because the zigzag stitch does not have a memory like a stretch-stitch does.

The following buttonhole is made with the overlock stitch on a reverse-action sewing machine. It can be made on any knit fabric from lightweight, interlock knits to the heaviest double knits, velours, and sweater knits. The stretch buttonhole keeps its shape no matter how much the garment is washed or worn and will never have that fishmouth appearance.

Stitch: . . . . Overlock stitch
Foot: . . . . Buttonhole foot or buttonhole foot with guide
Stitch length: . . Stretch-stitch or cam setting
Stitch width: . . 2 to 4mm.

Left Needle Position

1. Mark buttonholes as described on pages 72–74.

2. Set stitch width on 2mm and stitch down the first side of the buttonhole, stopping with the needle on the right side of the stitch.

3. Lift the presser foot and pivot the fabric 180°.

4. Put the presser foot down, take needle out of the work.

5. Set stitch length to 0mm., stitch width to 4mm., and bartack the end of the buttonhole a few stitches.

6. With the needle out of the work, set stitch length back to stretch-stitch or cam setting and the stitch width back to 2mm. Finish the second side of the buttonhole.

7. With needle out of the work, set stitch length to 0mm., stitch width to 4mm., and bartack a few stitches as before. Tie off buttonhole (figure 6-13).

Although this buttonhole has an open look to it, there is no need to stitch over it twice. *Hint:* Try this buttonhole with top-stitching thread on a woven blazer for a more handworked look to the buttonhole (figure 6-14).

Sheer Buttonhole

There are occasions when a conventional zigzag buttonhole is too heavy for a fine fabric, like tricot, crepe de chine, or sheer blouse-weight fabrics. You might want to make a button loop with a piece of elastic thread or ⅛-inch (3mm.) elastic braid set into the closure. If you have a

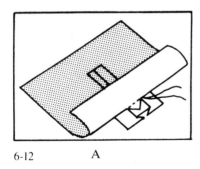

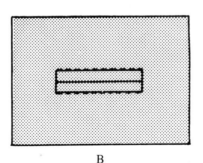

6-12   A   B

reverse-action sewing machine, you can either make a stretch buttonhole as previously described, or a sheer buttonhole for lightweight fabrics as follows:

Stitch: .... Picot stitch
Foot: .... Zigzag foot
Stitch length: .. Stretch-stitch or cam setting
Stitch width: .. 2mm.

1. Mark buttonhole length as described on pages 72-74.

2. Begin sewing the buttonhole with the picot stitch, and stop with the needle in the fabric on the right side of the stitch.

3. Lift the presser foot and pivot fabric 180°. Do not bartack.

4. Lower presser foot and stitch other side of buttonhole. Tie thread ends and carefully cut buttonhole open with a seam ripper (figure 6-15).

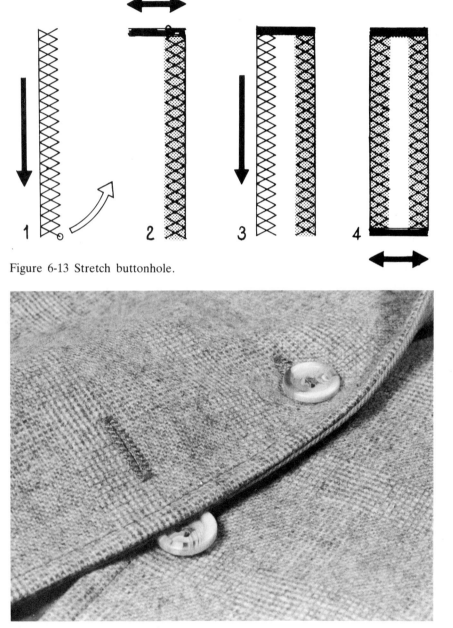

Figure 6-13 Stretch buttonhole.

Figure 6-14 Tailored stretch buttonhole.

Figure 6-15 Sheer buttonhole.

BUTTON SEWING

Although it is not in my contract, I am frequently asked to sew a button back on a jacket for someone at the office. Metal blazer buttons are the worst. As soon as I think I have found the best thread for the job, another button has to be sewn on. To make the next time you sew a metal blazer button on a jacket the last time, try this.

1. Look in your sewing basket and find all those looped eyelets that come in the package of hooks and eyes.

2. Thread one of the looped eyelets through the metal shank in the button. Sew the eyelet in place by hand with a double thread, buttonhole twist, or topstitching thread. The button shank wears against the metal eyelet, not the sewing thread (figure 6-16).

To sew on a two- or four-hole button by machine is easy. (It cannot be done on a straight-stitch machine, however.) Four-hole buttons can be sewn on in the conventional way, by crossing the threads, or by sewing two parallel bartacks. To be creative, however, machine stitch an arrow design and/or add hand French knots to make a flower (figure 6-17).

Figure 6-16 Button sewing with eyelet.

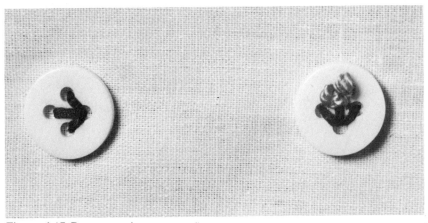

Figure 6-17 Button sewing: arrow, flower.

Zigzag Sewing Machine

Stitch: .... Zigzag stitch
Foot: .... Button-sewing foot (with or without shank maker)
Stitch length: .. 0mm. or drop feed dog
Stitch width: .. 2 to 4mm. depending on how far apart the holes in the button are.

This method is great when sewing a number of buttons on a garment.

1. Before sewing, tape button in place with a strip of cellophane tape or use a small piece of double-sided basting tape under the button. Test tape first

to make sure it will not harm your fabric.

2. For a thread shank, adjust the shank maker in the button-sewing foot where necessary. If using a button-sewing foot without a shank maker, place a toothpick or sewing machine needle on top of the button before taping.

3. Place the work under the button-sewing foot and take a couple of zigzag stitches, turning the flywheel by hand until the proper stitch width is set (figure 6-18). Sew enough zigzag stitches to attach button to the fabric.

4. Lift the presser foot and move the work to line up the needle with the second set of holes for a four-hole button. Stitch in place.

Figure 6-18 Button sewing with button-sewing foot.

5. Move the stitch width to 0mm. Taking care that the needle is over one of the holes, take a few straight stitches to lock off the stitches.

6. Remove work, leaving enough top thread to wrap around thread shank. Remove tape and/or toothpick.

7. Thread the top thread through one of the button's holes and wrap it around the thread shank between button and fabric. Pull excess thread to the wrong side and tie it off with the bobbin thread.

Reverse-Action Sewing Machine

Stitch: . . . . Overlock stitch
Foot: . . . . Button-sewing
foot
Stitch length: . . 0mm. or drop
feed dog
Stitch width: . . 2 to 4mm.

Prepare the work as described for the zigzag sewing machine, but instead of using a zigzag stitch, use the overlock stitch. This stitch takes two stitches in the left hole and one in the right hole. The stitches are automatically tied off by the machine. What a time-saver.

Chapter 7

RECYCLING OLD CLOTHES WITH A FLAIR

You can recycle almost anything these days: paper, aluminum cans, glass, egg cartons, and clothing. Form a partnership with your sewing machine for recycling as much as you can. It can be a very creative experience, as well as one that will save you money.

RECYCLING A SWEATER

Many ready-to-wear sweaters are made of beautiful, natural and synthetic yarns. When you are bored with them, but they are not ready for Goodwill, what do you do? Remake old sweaters into newer styles, or to fit someone else in the family. Here is how:

Layout, Cutting, and Shoulder Seams

1. Wash or clean the sweater.
2. Do not bother to rip the seams. Simply cut the sweater apart at the seams. Cut off ribbing at the neck, but do not cut off knitted-on ribbing at lower edges and wrists.
3. Press sweater pieces flat and block where necessary.
4. Lay out pattern pieces so the greatest stretch is around the body and cut new sweater with ¼-inch (6mm.) seam allowances. *Note:* If sweater has knitted-on ribbing, lay pattern out so ribbing is on the lower edge of sweater body and sleeves.
5. Using the knit seam finish recommended for your sewing machine, described on page 48, sew sweater together at the shoulder seams. Incorporate elastic thread in seams.

Ribbing

1. Decide on the finished width of the neckline ribbing, working with what you have from the old sweater. Double the *finished width* and add ½-inch (1.3cm.) for seam allowances. For a 1-inch (2.5cm.) wide finished ribbing, cut a 2½-inch (6.3cm.) wide strip, by the necessary length, as explained in the following step. *Note:* Some ribbing is finished on one side. If this is the case, cut ribbing the desired width plus ¼-inch (6mm.).
2. For a *crew neck,* measure the neckline opening and use two-thirds of the neckline opening measurement for the length of the ribbing.

For a V-*neck,* U-*neck, waistband,* or *cuff,* measure the opening and use three-fourths of the opening measurement for the ribbing length. You need longer ribbing in these areas to prevent it from creeping up on the neckline or strangling at the waistline or wrist.

A *cowl-neck* collar is used on a *U-neck sweater only* and is 12-inches (30.5cm.) wide. The collar measures the same length as the neckline opening. This way, it will drape well and will not bunch up around the neck. *Note:* Remember to cut cowl neck collar with the stretch going around the body.

3. After cutting the ribbing to size, seam it into a circle for every style except the cardigan. (Specific cardigan instructions are discussed on page 83).

4. Fold ribbing in half so the raw edges meet, and the seam is on the inside of the band.

If ribbing curls, baste raw edges together with a long, wide zigzag stitch. This makes the final stitching easier.

5. Divide the ribbing into four sections, marking with pins. Do the same for the garment opening. With right sides together, match pins and sew ribbing to garment with a ¼-inch (6mm.) seam. Check pages 44–50 for appropriate seam and seam finish. Ease the ribbing to the garment opening where needed.

6. Press ribbing, pressing seam toward garment, being careful not to stretch it out of shape. After ribbing is applied, you may want to topstitch under the seamline with the twin needle (figure 7-1). This gives a professional look to your handmade sweater.

7. Finish recycling your sweater by setting in the sleeves and sewing up the sleeve side seams. Hem the sweater as described on page 66. If ribbing is knitted into the hemline it will not be necessary to hem it.

This is a great way to get a little extra mileage out of an old sweater.

V-neck Cardigan Sweater Without Waistline Ribbing

1. Cut out your sweater as described above and stitch shoulder seams, incorporating elastic thread in seams (see page 48).

2. Pin up hem on sweater front, where ribbing will be sewn (figure 7-2).

3. Cut neckline ribbing desired width and slightly shorter than front opening measurement. Fold short ribbing end, right sides together, and stitch a ¼-inch (6mm.) seam; turn to right side and press. Repeat for other ribbing end. Apply neckline ribbing, pinning ribbing to sweater so it is eased into the neckline from one collar bone to the other. This way, the ribbing hugs the neckline (figure 7-2). Sew ¼-inch (6mm.) seam using appropriate seam finish.

4. Set in sleeves; stitch up sleeve and side seams with appropriate seam finish.

5. Apply ribbing to make cuffs, if necessary.

6. Hem sweater with stretch blind hem or twin needles (pages 64–66).

7. Make stretch buttonholes (page 78) and sew buttons on by hand with yarn that has been unraveled from the sweater knit.

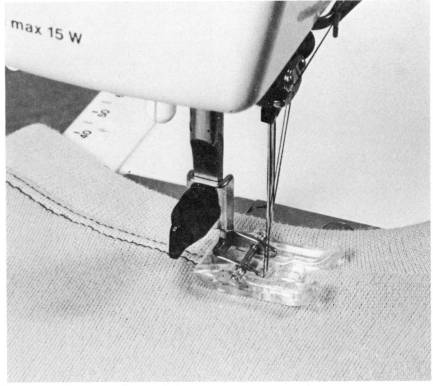

Figure 7-1 Twin-needle topstitch.

REMAKING GAUCHO PANTS INTO A SKIRT

If you have a pair of culottes or full-legged gaucho pants that you have worn only a few times, you might be able to recycle them into a wearable slim skirt. Candidates for restyling must have full legs, because there is more fabric to work with, making fitting easier (figure 7-3).

1. Rip crotch seam to approximately 9 inches (23cm.) below waistline. *Note:* If zipper is in center front or center back, rip crotch seam to ½-inch (1.3cm.) below bottom of zipper. Reinforce seam so it will not come unstitched. Take out hem.

2. Invite a friend over to help pin center-front and center-back seamlines. Try garment on, right sides out.

3. Overlap front pieces at center front and pin together, positioning pins to establish new seamline. Repeat for positioning of center-back seamline.

4. Take skirt off and mark seamline on center front and center back with felt-tip fabric marking pen or tailor's chalk (see page 39).

5. Repin with right sides together and baste center front. Trim away excess fabric, leaving generous seam allowances. Repeat for center back.

6. Gently press seam open and try skirt on again. Check to see that skirt flares properly in front and back.

7. Final stitch seams after fitting. Trim seam allowances to ⅝-inch (15mm.), and overcast as described in Chapter 5. Hem skirt. *Note:* If gaucho pants are lined, follow the procedure already described for lining, using the fabric trimmed away from center front and back crotch seams as a pattern for proper seam placement.

8. Press all seams open (figure 7-3).

RESTYLING A TENT DRESS

Do you own a dress you honestly think you like, but every time you put it on and belt the waistline, all the gathers arrange themselves where you do not want or need the fullness? Try restyling that dress by making an elastic casing or shirring in the waistline with elastic thread (figure 7-4).

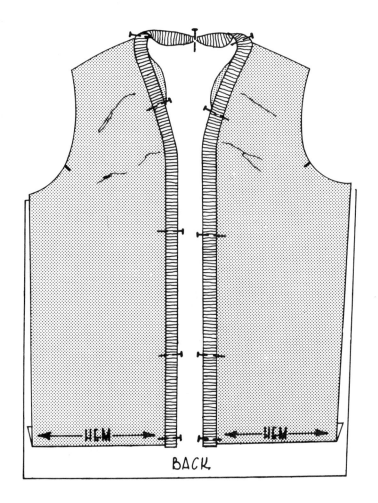

Figure 7-2 Ribbing application on a cardigan sweater.

Figure 7-3 Gaucho pants remade into a skirt.

Figure 7-4 Restyling a tent dress.

1. Try dress on, right side out.

2. Tie a narrow piece of elastic around your waist, arranging gathers evenly.

3. Have a friend mark elastic placement using a felt-tip fabric marking pen or tailor's chalk. *Note:* The ink will bleed through to the wrong side of the fabric, making positioning of the elastic casing or shirring much easier.

4. Make an elastic casing, or shir, in waistline as described on page 61.

If you accessorize your restyled dress with a fashionable belt, you may find you enjoy wearing it after all (figure 7-4).

RECYCLING PANTYHOSE

Do you have a collection of pantyhose with a run in only one leg? Here is a way to remake them into knee-highs or turn them into a new pair of hose by sewing two good legs together.

Knee-Highs

Zigzag Sewing Machine

Stitch Suggestions: Multistretch or interlock stitch

Foot: . . . . Embroidery foot
Stitch length: . . 1mm. or fine setting
Stitch width: . . 4mm.

Reverse-Action Sewing Machine

Stitch: . . . . Super-stretch stitch
Foot: . . . . Embroidery foot
Stitch length: . . Stretch-stitch or cam setting
Stitch width: . . 4mm.

1. Cut off elastic from the top of pantyhose. If elastic is knitted into the waistband, use a piece of nonroll elastic and measure it to fit comfortably around your calves allowing an extra ½-inch (1.3cm.) for seam. *Note:* If you have varicose veins you can finally wear a custom-made pair of knee highs that will not strangle your legs.

2. Seam elastic into a circle, overlapping the ends, and sew around all four sides of the overlap, forming a box. Use a tiny zigzag stitch (1mm. stitch length or fine setting, 1mm. stitch width) to do this.

3. Before cutting off hose, try them on your leg. Cut them at least 1 inch (2.5cm.) longer than needed so elastic can be encased in the nylon fabric. *Note:* If you use a wide elastic, be sure you have enough pantyhose nylon to encase elastic.

4. Pin elastic into nylon, folding fabric down under the elastic and encasing it so the raw edges of the nylon are tucked under elastic (figure 7-5).

5. Using the recommended stitch for your machine, sew elastic into place so the stitch is slightly off the elastic on the left and catches into the elastic on the right (figure 7-5). This way, the elastic will lie flat against your leg.

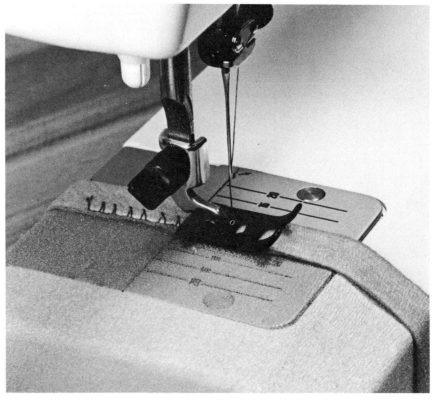

Figure 7-5 Making knee-highs.

Sewing Two Good Legs Together

Zigzag Sewing Machine

Stitch Suggestions: Multistretch or interlock stitch

Foot: . . . . Embroidery foot
Stitch length: . . 1mm. or fine setting
Stitch width: . . 4mm.

Reverse-Action Sewing Machine

Stitch Suggestions: Double overlock or super-stretch stitch

Foot: . . . . Embroidery foot
Stitch length: . . Stretch-stitch or cam setting
Stitch width: . . 4mm.

This method only works with pantyhose that have a knitted-in elastic waistband.

1. Cut pantyhose apart, starting at the waist, going down through the crotch, and cutting away the seam allowance. If your pantyhose has a gusset crotch, cut straight through it.
2. Pin two good legs, right sides together, matching elastic at waist.
3. Using the recommended stitch, sew legs together (starting at the waistline), guiding the work so the needle bites into fabric on the left, and swings off raw edge at the right (figure 7-6).

Mending Sock Tops

Do not be caught with your socks down. Putting the stretch back into sock tops sure beats holding them up with rubber bands.

Zigzag Sewing Machine

Stitch Suggestions: Interlock, multistretch or multiple-zigzag stitch

Foot: . . . . Embroidery foot
Stitch length: . . 1mm. or fine setting
Stitch width: . . 4mm.

Reverse-Action Sewing Machine

Stitch: . . . . Double overlock stitch
Foot: . . . . Embroidery foot
Stitch length: . . Stretch-stitch or cam setting
Stitch width: . . 4mm.

1. Buy a good grade of elastic thread with a high cotton-fiber content.

2. Place sock top and a double strand of elastic thread under presser foot so the needle bites into the fabric on the left and swings over elastic thread onto the fabric and off the edge at the right (figure 7-7). *Note:* Do not pull on elastic thread when sewing, as this may cause it to be too tight after the sock has been mended.

LENGTHENING HEMLINES

One of the most unpredictable fashion trends is hem length. One year it is 3 inches above the knee, the next it is 3 inches below the knee. To stretch your wardrobe and still be fashionable, let the existing hemline down and

Figure 7-6 Recycling pantyhose.

face the edge, or add a hemline of matching or contrasting fabric.

When letting a hem down, the problem is usually pressing out the old hemline. Try using equal parts of white vinegar and water on a press cloth, then press hem with hot iron. If the fabric has faded, as most likely will happen to denim or corduroy, you may want to disguise the hemline with reverse-machine embroidery.

Straight-Stitch Sewing Machine

Stitch: . . . . Straight stitch
Foot: . . . . Straight-stitch foot
Stitch length: . . 4mm. or 6 stitches per inch

Zigzag Sewing Machine

Stitch Suggestions: Zigzag, ball, diamond, domino, or checker stitch

Foot: . . . . Embroidery foot
Stitch length: . . ¾ to 1mm. or fine setting
Stitch width: . . 4mm.

Reverse-Action Sewing Machine

Stitch Suggestions: Feather, leaf, wave, or smocking stitch

Foot: . . . . Embroidery foot
Stitch length: . . Stretch-stitch or cam setting
Stitch width: . . 4mm.

1. Prepare your machine as described on pages 116–118 for reverse-machine embroidery.

2. On the wrong side of the garment, mark a line where embroidery stitching will be sewn. An old hemline may be suffi-

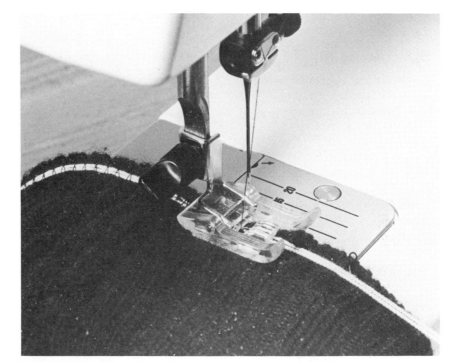

Figure 7-7 Mending sock tops.

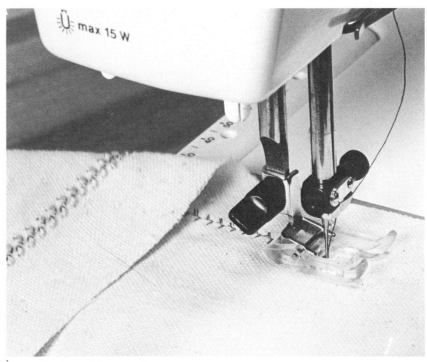

Figure 7-8 Disguising hemline.

89

ciently visible on the wrong side to use.

3. With the wrong side up, sew over the line with the decorative stitch. The stitch camouflages the hemline (figure 7-8). *Note:* So it is not apparent that the hemline has been camouflaged, decorate the sleeves, pocket, or collar with the same stitch. Or you can make several rows of stitching above the first. You may like the new styling better than when the garment was new.

NARROW FAGOTTING

Fagotting is a way of joining two pieces of fabric with visible, decorative stitching. If you have a straight-stitch sewing machine, fagotting trim is available by the yard and can be stitched between the body of the garment and the hem. If you have a zigzag or reverse-action sewing machine, fagotting can be done with regular sewing thread, pearl cotton, or embroidery floss in the bobbin. Use fagotting to pep up an old dress or blouse. Run a row of it across the upper bodice, down each side of the center front, near a sleeve or garment hem—wherever an old garment needs a lift.

Zigzag Sewing Machine
Method 1

Stitch: . . . . Multiple-zigzag stitch
Foot: . . . . Embroidery foot
Stitch length: . . 1½mm. or 20 stitches per inch
Stitch width: . . 4mm.

Method 2

Stitch: . . . . Zigzag stitch
Foot: . . . . Fringe foot
Stitch length: . . ½mm. or fine setting
Stitch width: . . 4mm.

Regular sewing thread in bobbin, loosened upper tension.

Reverse-Action Sewing Machine

Stitch: . . . . Featherstitch
Foot: . . . . Embroidery foot
Stitch length: . . Stretch-stitch or cam setting
Stitch width: . . 4mm.

1. Thread machine with regular sewing thread for a delicate look, or thread bobbin with pearl cotton as for reverse-machine embroidery described on page 116, for a hand-crocheted look.

2. Cut apart or let hem down on garment where fagotting will be done.

3. Press the two fabric edges under ¼-inch (6mm.) that will be fagotted together.

4. With wrong side up, place both folded edges under the presser foot as shown, leaving about a ⅛-inch (3mm.) space between them (figure 7-9).

5. Begin sewing. Without watching the needle, guide the work so the space between the two fabric edges is even. The needle takes a stitch on one piece of fabric, a stitch through the space in the middle, then

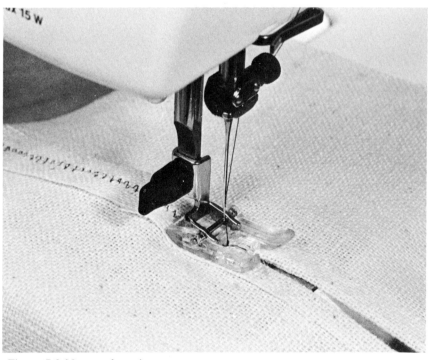

Figure 7-9 Narrow fagotting.

swings over to the other piece of fabric and joins it to the first. This seam is decorative, functional, and can give much more wear and interest to a favorite garment.

WIDE FAGOTTING

There are many decorative stitches that can be used to join two pieces of fabric together. The following is another method of fagotting with a reverse-action sewing machine. The decorative work is wider and more interesting than in previously discussed techniques. Adding-machine tape is used under the stitching to stabilize and maintain even stitches (figure 7-10).

Reverse-Action Sewing Machine

Stitch: .... Super-stretch stitch
Foot: .... Embroidery foot
Stitch length:.. Stretch-stitch or cam setting
Stitch width: .. 4mm.

1. Prepare the machine for reverse-machine embroidery as described on pages 116–118.
2. Press the two fabric edges under ¼-inch (6mm.) that will be fagotted together.
3. With the wrong side up, and adding-machine tape under the work, place the folded edge of one piece of fabric partly under the foot. The needle must stitch in the fabric at the right and swing off onto the paper at the left.

4. After the first row of stitching is complete, turn the work around. With the wrong side up, place folded edge of the second piece of fabric under the foot as before. The needle must stitch on the fabric at the right and swing onto the paper over previous stitching at the left. The two pieces of fabric are joined by stitching. The paper keeps the stitches uniform (figure 7-10).

5. Carefully rip the paper away from the stitching with tweezers. *Note:* Wet the paper for easy removal. Many other stitches can be used the same way (figure 7-11). Try different stitches on your machine to see what interesting effects you can create.

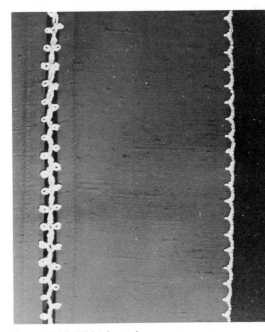

Figure 7-10 Wide fagotting.

Figure 7-11 Finished wide fagotting.

MENDING

Mending is one of the necessary evils of sewing, but it does not have to be time-consuming and tedious.

A free-arm sewing machine is ideal for mending because it is designed to reach those hard-to-repair areas, such as knees and elbows. With a flat-bed machine, mending is not as easy, but there are a few areas that can be mended by moving the fabric freehand without the foot pressure and/or presser foot. It can be done on any type of sewing machine.

Freehand Darning

Darning by machine is done without a presser foot, using the straight-stitch setting. Drop or cover feed dog and set stitch width on 0mm.

1. Place the area to be mended into an embroidery hoop.
2. Place the fabric under the needle and stitch a circle around the hole, drawing any raveled threads into the middle of the hole.
3. Begin moving the work slowly back and forth under the needle (figure 7-12).
4. After the lengthwise threads have been sewn, move the work from side to side under the needle. In no time, the hole is mended. *Hint:* To mend denim jeans, use a gray thread on the bobbin and a navy thread on top. Loosen the upper tension. The bobbin thread will slightly pull up to the top of the work,

giving an almost invisible mend. After mending, return tension to normal setting.

Patching

You can use matching or contrasting fabrics for patching. The most important thing is to use a fabric similar in weight and type to the garment.

Straight-Stitch Sewing Machine

Stitch: . . . . Straight stitch
Foot: . . . . Straight-stitch foot
Stitch length: . . 0mm., drop feed dog or cover feed with darning plate

Release the pressure on your machine, and drop the feed dog to the *down* position. You will be moving the fabric under the needle by hand.

1. Press under the raw edges of the patch ⅛–¼-inch (3-6mm.), and pin the patch in place.
2. Place the work under the presser foot. Begin stitching close to the edge of the patch. *Hint:* Hold the garment firmly for even stitching. You may have to put the work in a hoop to keep it stable.
3. Move work slowly under the needle until the patch is sewn in place. This way, you can stitch around all four sides of the patch without turning the garment.

Figure 7-12 Freestyle darning.

Zigzag and Reverse-Action Sewing Machines

Method 1 (figure 7-13)

Stitch: . . . . Zigzag stitch
Foot: . . . . Embroidery foot
Stitch length: . . ½ to ¾mm. or fine setting
Stitch width: . . 4mm.

Method 2 (figure 7-14)

Stitch: . . . . Multiple-zigzag stitch
Foot: . . . . Zigzag or embroidery foot
Stitch length: . . ½ to ¾mm. or fine setting
Stitch width: . . 4mm.

1. Turn under the raw edges of the patch ¼ to ⅛-inch (6–3mm.) if you are using the zigzag stitch, and pin patch in place. *Note:* Unlike the ordinary zigzag stitch, made with 2 stitches from side to side, the multiple-zigzag stitch has 6 to 10 stitches that keeps fabric flat. This stitch is great for overcasting raveling fabric edges and can be used to patch and mend without having to turn under the raw edges on a patch.

2. Place the work under the foot so the needle swings half on the patch and half on the garment.

3. Stitch down one side of patch and pivot the work. Stitch down second side of patch, reinforcing the work with extra stitches at the corner.

4. Pivot again and sew the third side of the patch, using the instant- or continuous-reverse on the machine, if you have this feature, to feed the fabric backward (figure 7-13, 7-14).

Figure 7-13 Patching with the zigzag stitch (method 1).

Figure 7-14 Patching with the multiple-zigzag stitch (method 2).

5. Pivot the fabric again, reinforcing the corner, and continue sewing backward. This technique is a real time and temper saver.

Mending Knit Fabrics

Your zigzag or reverse-action machine easily mends all types of knits. While knits do not tend to tear as wovens do, it is important to know that you can easily mend cuts or runs in knits.

Zigzag Sewing Machine

Stitch: .... Multiple-zigzag
                stitch
Foot: .... Zigzag or
                embroidery foot
Stitch length:.. ¾mm. or fine
                setting
Stitch width: .. 4mm.

Reverse-Action Sewing Machine

Stitch: .... Smocking stitch
Foot: .... Zigzag or
                embroidery foot
Stitch length:.. Stretch-stitch or
                cam setting
Stitch width: .. 4mm.

1. Place the rip, run, or tear under the presser foot, centering the worn area under the foot (figure 7-15).
2. Begin sewing. Both the multiple-zigzag and the smocking stitch are preferred over the zigzag stitch, because they keep the fabric flat and allow the mended area to stretch after it has been repaired. *Note:* If the area is badly torn, you may also patch the fabric using the multiple-zigzag stitch or smocking stitch as described on pages 15 and 20.

RECYCLING FUR

Fur provides the warmest protection against winter weather and wears much better than cloth. The hairs of a natural fur stand up in the cold weather and trap warm air between them to insulate against winter's cold. Although fur is not as readily available as fabric, there are a number of places you can find fur that will not cost you a fortune.

Furriers, dry cleaners, and lay-away departments in department stores often have storage facilities that have unclaimed furs to sell for reasonable prices. You may also find a variety of used furs at thrift shops, flea markets,

and estate sales. But caution must be exercised. Although the fur may look acceptable from the right side, loosen the lining and inspect the pelts.

The leather on the back of the pelts should be soft, supple, and fairly thick, and the fur should have few bald spots. For further information on the fur, have it validated by a reputable furrier, and try to get a garment large enough to accommodate ripping apart for restyling.

The best types of fur for recycling are muskrat, mink, lamb, raccoon, fox, or wolf. These furs have thick skins and are durable enough to withstand restyling. *Note:* Although there are many good resources for second-hand

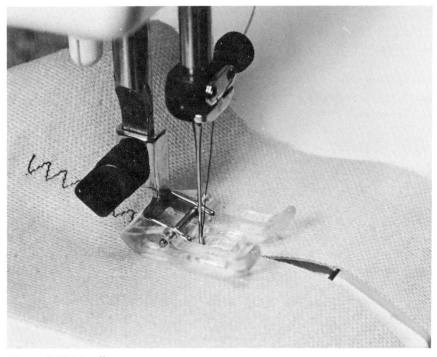

Figure 7-15 Mending a tear.

furs, you may want to work with a synthetic fur. It is easy to care for, is more readily available than real fur, and often provides more warmth than cloth. The cutting and construction techniques are the same for both fur and furlike fabric.

Construction and Reconstruction

Before restyling, cut the old lining out of the coat. For the most professional look, the new lining should be made of satin underlined with outing flannel. Before sewing the lining in the new coat, add a customized touch. Monogram it as described on page 107 or have it professionally monogrammed for a

more ready-to-wear look.

After removing the lining, cut out the sleeves and open the shoulder seams so the fur is flat. Locate and mark a center-back line with a felt-tip pen. When cutting the fur apart, cut from the wrong side with a razor blade or Exacto knife (figure 7-16). After the coat has been cut apart, see how much fur you have to work with and choose a pattern.

The pattern should be very simple and cut full through the shoulders. This area gets the most stress. By cutting it wider across the shoulders, the pelts will not stretch, avoiding damage to the fur. If the pattern is not designed this way, make necessary adjustments to tissue pattern

piece. To make your pattern layout easier, mark pelts with a grainline, using a felt-tip pen. Tape pattern pieces to the pelt, overlapping side seams (at the seamline) as shown. Cut out one side and half of back, then flip over pattern on the center-back line and cut remaining half. The sleeves can be cut in two parts, if necessary, with the undersleeve made of leather or synthetic suede. This way, the fur on the body of coat will not rub off under the sleeve. If you are running short of fur, you can make leather or synthetic suede insets on the side of the coat under the sleeve as well. After pattern pieces have been cut, label them with a felt-tip pen. *Note:* Re-

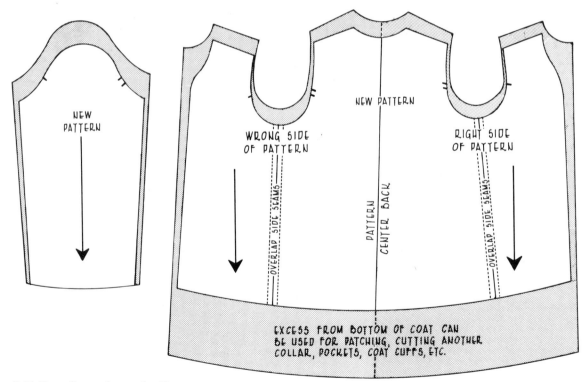

Figure 7-16 Recycling a fur or fur-like coat.

member to cut both right and left sides. Cut one side with the right side of the pattern facing up, the other side with the pattern facing down. You would not want to have two left sleeves when you are finished.

Before sewing, reinforce areas of stress with rows of ¼-inch (6mm.) twill tape. This can be attached quickly, using a hand whipstitch and a hand-needle for leather. Do not sew the tape on by machine. Again, the most important area to reinforce is across the shoulders and the broadest part of the back (figure 7-17).

Sewing fur and furlike fabrics requires an almost invisible seam. Providing the pelts are in good shape, furs can be remade a number of times. Furriers have sewing machines that join pelts with an invisible seam, made with a curved needle and a loose thread tension. We can create almost the same effect with a domestic sewing machine and a zigzag stitch.

You can sew fur and furlike fabrics with excellent results on your sewing machine.

Zigzag and Reverse-Action Sewing Machines

Stitch: . . . . Zigzag stitch
Foot: . . . . Zigzag foot
Stitch length: . . ½mm. or fine setting
Stitch width: . . 2 to 3mm.

1. Thread machine with 100 percent cotton or silk thread and an American size 11, or European size 70, all-purpose or sharp sewing machine needle.

2. Loosen the upper tension. If your tension is marked from 0 to 9, set it at about 2. If your tension is marked "Tight, Normal, Loose," set in on "Loose."

3. Place the right sides together, pushing all the nap away from the seam. Use paper clips or bobby pins to keep the skins together.

4. Place raw edge halfway under the presser foot so the needle bites into the pelt on the left and swings off the edge at the right. After completing a seam, pull gently on the pelt so the stitching on the back is flat, and the fur or pile can be pulled up out of the seam. The seam should be invisible from the right side of the work (figure 7-18).

5. When sewing a leather or synthetic-suede inset into a coat

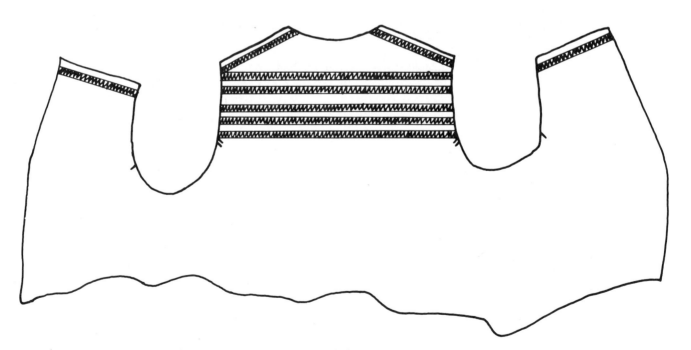

Figure 7-17 Reinforce stress areas and across the back with twill-tape.

or sleeve, follow the same procedure. You may have to pull fur or pile up through the stitching with the help of a hand-needle. *Note:* Fur can be sewn together in almost any direction as long as there is not a definite pattern in the fur. To piece it, cut away the bad part of the pelt from the skin side and replace it with a more substantial piece of fur. The sewing technique is the same as described above.

After pelts have been sewn together, sew in the lining by hand. Hemming the fur must be done by hand as well, using an invisible whipstitch.

Do's and Don'ts About Fur

After your garment is complete, treat it with tender loving care.

Do put your fur in cold storage. This makes the fur stand up as it did on the animal, and it will retain all its natural thickness and shine.

Do hang your fur on a wooden hanger. This better supports the weight of the coat and is kinder to the shoulder seams and back.

Do store your fur in a porous garment bag when traveling. This protects the garment and also allows it to breathe. *Note:* A garment bag can be made from old cotton pillowcases or sheets.

Do enjoy all the luxury, warmth, and wear you will get from your remade fur or furlike coat.

Don't spray on perfume or hair spray while wearing the fur. The alcohol dries out the skin under the fur, and could cause it to crack and split.

Don't store fur in mothballs. This dries out the leather, and the fur absorbs the odor.

Don't pin a corsage or jewelry to the fur. This pokes holes and breaks down the leather pelt.

Don't carry a shoulder bag, because the strap will wear away the fur, and the weight of the purse may weaken shoulder seams.

Avoid carrying boxes and luggage while wearing fur. This may cause unnecessary balding of the fur and stress on the seams.

Figure 7-18 Stitching fur.

Chapter 8

RAGS TO RICHES WITH STITCHES

When I first went into the home-sewing industry, I thought I would be forced to decorate everything from lingerie to business suits with little ducks and fish. I didn't care if I had to compromise my principles of good taste—I needed the job. Fortunately, my later experience introduced me to many elegant applications of decorative stitches and machine embroidery—the most dramatic trend felt by both ready-to-wear and home-sewing industries in recent years.

Embroidery opens a new world of sewing pleasure and has touched the lives of even the most unlikely candidates. A sewing machine dealer I once knew sold sewing machines and C.B. radios, an odd combination, but at a stop light on Rural Route 1, what do you expect? The owners of the shop had to have names,

or handles, to broadcast over the airwaves and decided on "Super A-One Ace" and "Rosebud." Super A-One Ace would call his good buddies on Channel 9 and invite them to stop at the store so Rosebud could machine-embroider their handles on the backs of their jackets or in other choice locations. Did business improve!

Appliqué, freehand embroidery, decorative stitching, and the use of machine accessories are common ways to make handmade or ready-to-wear garments and linens unique. Tasteful machine embroidery expresses your personality and is quickly completed, unlike hand embroidery. The only stumbling block that has prevented some sewers from trying machine embroidery seems to be the lack of new ideas.

I have been told by hundreds of sewers that they just are not

creative. I wish I could say that I dreamed up some great embroidery ideas on my own, too, but when I need an idea, I borrow it.

Look around you. Everything from newspapers to children's coloring books abound with art forms that can be interpreted in embroidery. Many idea books that include iron-on transfers and other easy-to-duplicate designs are available. Recently a friend enlarged a picture she found on a greeting card and made it into a lovely wall hanging. Mail-order catalogs also have ideas that can be adapted to your needs. No matter where ideas come from, there always seem to be more than I have time to use. I have an overflowing clipping file I constantly refer to for inspiration.

After the inspiration, decide on your interpretation of the design—color scheme, texture of

Figure 8-1 Machine embroidery supplies.

thread, and fabric. Good sources for fabric are remnant tables in stores and your fabric scrap box at home. I have found some great threads and fabrics at yard sales and rummage sales, too. Use your imagination, and be sure to use the right tools for best results.

Whenever you are embroidering by machine, equipment must be in top working order. The sewing machine must be well oiled and oiled more frequently (approximately every four to six hours of sewing time) than for normal sewing. Be sure your machine has a new needle in it, preferably an American size 11 or European size 80. The area under the feed dog must also be lint free for perfect stitch formation. Refer to page 137 for information on sewing machine care.

Fabrics most suitable for machine embroidery are made of natural fibers, such as cotton, silk, wool, and linen. If you cannot find fabrics of natural fibers, choose a blend that is firmly woven and has a high, natural-fiber content. Unbleached muslin, chintz, khaki, poplin, and lightweight denim are types of fabrics that work well. Remember to preshrink the fabric whenever possible to wash out any sizing that may cause skipped stitches. If you will not be washing your project, such as a wall hanging, the best fabric to use is felt. It is not woven, so there is no grain to distort the stitching, as may happen with other fabrics. Unwanted puckers in felt also steam out easily. After choosing the fabric, the next area

of interest is threads.

There are threads made of cotton fibers, some of 100 percent polyester, nylon, or rayon. There are many that are combinations. With so many choices, which one works the best? For embroidery, I prefer cotton thread for decorative work on clothing and rayon thread for wall hangings.

Cotton threads are widely available, can be used with decorative stitches, and keep their luster and durability throughout many washings. Rayon threads are more difficult to find, have a higher sheen, and are finer than cotton threads. Both have their advantages. Test to find the one that works the best for you.

Other threads, such as embroidery floss, pearl cotton, metallic threads, yarn, and cordonnet (commonly used for hand crochet) can also be used to create special embroidered effects. Whenever I am on the road, I like to investigate craft and yarn stores to see what might be interesting to use on my sewing machine. I once used rayon floss I found in a bait store in Michigan for topstitching. Fishermen use it to tie their flies. I also found that ⅛-inch (3mm.) silk ribbon used for hand crocheting can be used in the bobbin for reverse-machine embroidery (page 116).

To do machine embroidery easily, fabrics should be placed in an embroidery hoop or *frame,* as it is sometimes called. I found a spring-wire hoop I like that is about six inches in diameter. It does not bump into the machine, and the sides are thin enough to

fit under the needle without taking the needle out of the machine. If you prefer using a metal or plastic hoop, wrap the inside ring with twill tape. The textured ring will keep fabric taut in the hoop while sewing. Embroidery hoops and other specialty equipment are available in sewing machine stores, and specialty fabric and needlework shops. Other supplies you will need include a sharp pair of embroidery scissors, cellophane tape, tweezers, tissue paper, adding-machine tape, typing paper, woven interfacing, and/or synthetic or silk organza used under the work to prevent puckering on lightweight fabrics (figure 8-1). Now that you are prepared with fabric, threads, and supplies, you must learn how to transfer the design onto the fabric.

BASIC PATTERN TRANSFER

There are many ways to transfer a design onto the background fabric with the use of hot transfer patterns, transfer pencils, etc., but I prefer transferring the design by stitching it onto the fabric. It is the easiest method to use for both machine appliqué and embroidery. The following works well for all types of sewing machines.

Stitch: . . . . Straight stitch
Foot: . . . . None
Stitch length: . . 0mm., drop feed dog or cover feed with darning plate
Stitch width: . . 0mm.

1. Trace the design on a piece of tissue paper and pin the paper to the fabric.

2. Place the work, stretched drum-tight in a hoop, under the needle, and lower the presser bar. *Note:* Be careful not to tear the tissue pattern while stretching fabric in hoop. Machine should be threaded with slightly contrasting top and bobbin thread.

3. Holding the top thread in your left hand, turn the flywheel once until the bobbin thread comes up through the fabric. Pull bobbin thread up.

4. Take a few locking stitches, and clip threads off at the fabric (figure 8-2).

5. Begin outlining the design, including all the detail. The nee-dle should sound like a beating drum as it stitches in and out of the tissue paper and fabric.

6. Rip the paper away after stitching. A permanent design is transferred to the work that will not wash or steam out.

After transferring the design to the fabric, you are ready to start the embroidery. We will start with something familiar to most sewers, appliqué.

Appliqué

Most sewers make a lot of trouble for themselves when try-ing to appliqué. Usually they cut many shapes and try to piece them together like a puzzle. The problem is that the appliqué of-ten pulls away from the stitches after a few washings. The best way to appliqué is to think of the design in its proper perspec-tive—that is, the area farthest away from you is the first piece to be applied to the background fabric. In most cases, this means that the larger parts of the appli-qué are applied first, followed by the smaller, detail sections. With this method, you could consider the appliqué to be layered rather than pieced. The following in-structions are for all types of sewing machines.

Stitch: . . . . Straight stitch
Foot: . . . . Straight-stitch or embroidery foot
Stitch length: . . 1 to 1½mm. or fine setting
Stitch width: . . 0mm.

1. Transfer detailed appliqué design onto background fabric, as described in previous section, pages 100–101. Transfer stitches will be visible as design outlines, on both right and wrong sides of work.

2. Tape a large piece of appli-qué fabric onto the right side of background fabric. Remember that the first piece appliquéd is the one that is undermost and looks like it is farthest away from you.

3. *From the wrong side,* use a short, straight stitch and sew around the shape that is being appliquéd, using transfer stitches as a guide.

4. After completing the shape, turn work over to the right side and trim the excess fabric from around the stitched shape with sharp embroidery scissors.

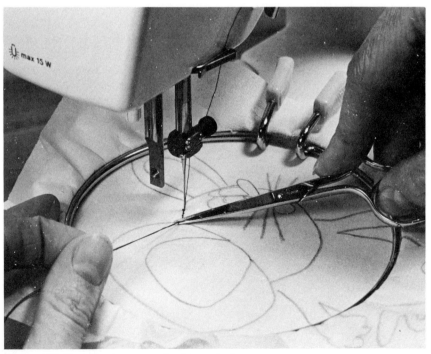
Figure 8-2 Transferring an embroidery design.

Figure 8-3 Appliqué progression (step 6).

5. Topstitch the shape with a stitch appropriate for your machine (see next section, pages 102–104).

6. Appliqué each shape, one at a time, as previously described, until design is complete (figure 8-3).

Appliqué Topstitch

Topstitching the shapes in place can be a creative use of the decorative stitches built in to your machine. The following are a few ideas that may help to better utilize the stitches available to you.

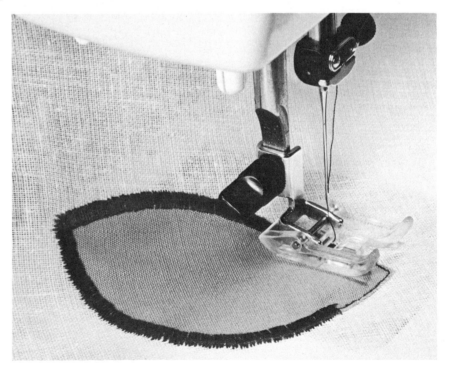

Figure 8-4 Topstiching an appliqué.

Straight-Stitch Sewing Machine

You do not have a satin stitch or other decorative stitch built in to your machine; so topstitching the appliqué must be done by hand. The satin stitch sewn with a strand or two of embroidery floss is the easiest and most common way to topstitch an appliqué, but have you ever thought of using a hand buttonhole stitch or chain stitch? These stitches are secure and add interest to the appliqué. To experiment with other hand stitches, you can get some ideas from looking at the decorative stitches built in on newer sewing machines. They are easily duplicated by hand.

Zigzag Sewing Machine

The most common way to topstitch an appliqué is with the satin stitch.

Stitch: .... Satin stitch (zigzag stitch)
Foot: .... Embroidery foot
Stitch length:.. ¼ to ½mm. or fine setting
Stitch width: .. 2 to 4mm.

The satin stitch can be used on most any shape. I like to use a narrower stitch width on small shapes and a wider stitch width on large shapes. When turning a curve or sharp corner, sew very slowly. The stitches on the inside of the curve should meet in the same needle hole so the stitches on the outside of the curve fan out. This will prevent unnecessary pile-up of stitches at the corner of the shape (figure 8-4).

Figure 8-5 Picot stitch on a finished appliqué.

103

Never think the satin stitch is your only possibility, however. Stitches in the shape of a ball, diamond, scallop, or domino—made by varying the zigzag stitch width—secure the appliqué and give a creative treatment, adding another dimension to decorative sewing.

Reverse-Action Sewing Machine

Your sewing machine can do all the preceding techniques for machine appliqué, plus many more suitable stitches used on a wider variety of fabrics. One of the stitches I like the best is the following:

Stitch: . . . . Picot stitch
Foot: . . . . Embroidery or
                 zigzag foot
Stitch length: . . Stretch-stitch or
                 cam setting
Stitch width: . . 2mm.

This fine and very secure stitch can be used on most fabrics from the lightest silks and Qiana to loftier napped velveteen and velour. In figure 8-5, the picot stitch is used to appliqué the mouse to the background fabric. This stitch gives a clean finish to the edge of the appliqué because the stitches bury themselves in both the appliqué and background fabric. Keep in mind that this stitch is also great for lace appliqués on nylon tricot and other fine fabrics. However, it is not the only stitch suitable for appliqué. Experiment with other decorative stitches as shown in figures 8-6 A & B and figure 8-7.

Figures 8-6a & b Appliqué motifs.

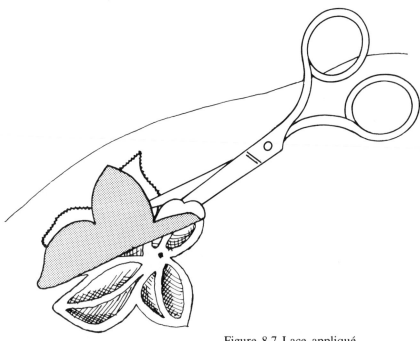

Figure 8-7 Lace appliqué.

Lace Appliqué

There are many types of lace available for lingerie and outerwear. With some, it is difficult to distinguish the right from the wrong side. Examine lace closely. The right side has heavier threads defining the design. To appliqué lace, prepare your machine as follows:

Straight-Stitch Sewing Machine

Stitch: . . . . Straight stitch
Foot: . . . . Straight-stitch foot
Stitch length: . . 1 to 1½mm. or fine setting

Zigzag Sewing Machine

Stitch: . . . . Zigzag stitch
Foot: . . . . Zigzag or embroidery foot
Stitch length . . 1mm. or fine setting
Stitch width: . . 1mm.

Reverse-Action Sewing Machine

Stitch: . . . . Picot stitch
Foot: . . . . Zigzag or embroidery foot
Stitch length: . . Stretch-stitch or cam setting
Stitch width: . . 2mm.

1. Choose lace section for the appliqué and cut it out, leaving excess fabric around the design.
2. Tape or pin lace where desired to the right side of your work.

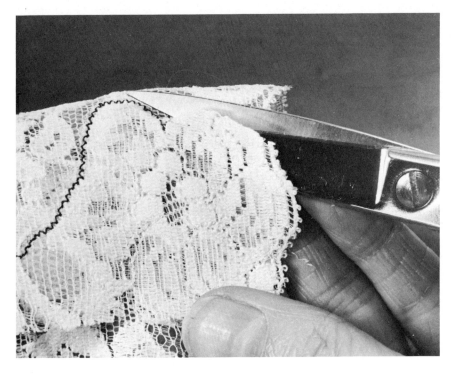

Figure 8-8 Lace seams.

106

3. Using the appropriate stitch, stitch around the shape. Do not sew over tape; remove pins as you reach them; tie off thread ends.

4. From the right side of work, trim excess lace close to stitching.

Lace Cutwork

Lace cutwork creates excitement in handmade lingerie. Simply follow the foregoing instructions for lace appliqué, then trim away the fabric from behind the appliqué with a sharp pair of embroidery scissors (figure 8-7).

Lace Seams

The following technique practically fuses lace together invisibly. It is for zigzag and reverse-action machines only. For a straight-stitch machine, overcast design by hand.

Stitch: . . . . Zigzag stitch
Foot: . . . . Zigzag or
                embroidery foot
Stitch length: . . 1mm. or fine
                setting
Stitch width: . . 1mm.

1. Measure lace the desired length, leaving extra lace at both ends.

2. Overlap lace ends, matching the design or scallops at the edge and stitch over heavier design lines with a small zigzag stitch.

3. Trim excess lace from both sides of the seam (figure 8-8).

When using matching threads, the seam almost disappears.

MONOGRAMMING

One of the first things I wanted to learn when I got my new sewing machine was how to monogram. I went for my lesson, and after practicing, I was able to make my initial—on that stiff fabric tunneled under the stitch, demonstrations. I went home and tried monogramming one of my mother's dish towels. After much effort, I gave up, because the fabric tunneled under the stitch, resulting in a puckered mess. Here are a few tips that will save you from a similar bad experience.

There are two different ways to monogram, either freehand or by using the presser foot. Freehand monogramming is where the fabric is moved by hand under the needle without the use of a presser foot. The method you use depends on the stitch and style of the monogram. For example, a monogram made in a bouclé stitch is done freehand, while a tapered or block monogram is made with the zigzag stitch and use of the embroidery foot. In either case, the fabric selection and preparation of the work is the same.

Firmly woven fabrics are most suitable for monogramming and must be stretched drum tight in an embroidery hoop. If, after testing, the fabric is puckering, place a piece of paper or interfacing under the work. Knits are not usually recommended for monogramming, but can be used by experienced sewers if the work is backed with a stable, woven interfacing.

Bouclé Monograms

One of the daintiest monograms can be made with all types of sewing machines. The technique is called *bouclé* stitching. It means small cord stitch, because it looks like a piece of cording is sewn in place to create the monogram.

Bouclé stitching is done by changing both upper and lower thread tensions. If your machine *does not* have a bobbin case with a tension by-pass hole, invest in a second bobbin case to experiment with bobbin tensions (figure 8-9).

Stitch: . . . . Straight stitch
Foot: . . . . None
Stitch length: . . 0mm. drop feed
                dog or cover
                feed with darning
                plate
Stitch width: . . 0mm.

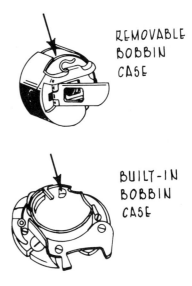

REMOVABLE BOBBIN CASE

BUILT-IN BOBBIN CASE

Figure 8-9 By-pass bobbin tension.

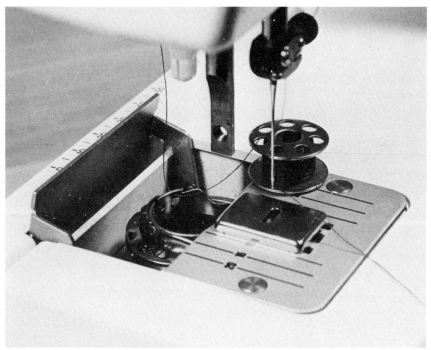

Figure 8-10 By-pass bobbin tension.

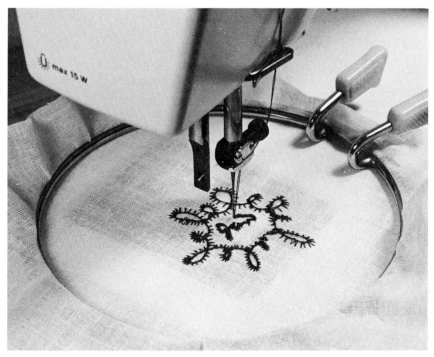

Figure 8-11 Bouclé monogram.

1. Thread the top with two threads through the same needle (American size 11 or European size 80). Thread bobbin with matching threads.

2. Either by-pass bobbin tension (figure 8-10), or loosen the tension screw on the bobbin case so there is just a slight drag on the bobbin thread.

3. With the work stretched drum tight in the embroidery hoop, place the work under the needle and lower the presser bar.

4. Holding the upper thread end in your left hand, turn the flywheel with your right so the needle picks up the bobbin thread. Bring bobbin thread through the fabric and take a couple of locking stitches. Cut thread ends off at the fabric so they will not get caught in the work.

5. Begin sewing by moving the machine quickly and your hands slowly. The bobbin thread is pulled up to the surface of the fabric, covering the upper threads (figure 8-11).

Practice moving the fabric under the needle in controlled curves. Once this technique is mastered, monogramming is as easy as moving a piece of paper under a stationary pen. *Note:* By stitching *slowly* and moving your hands *quickly,* you will create an effect called *spark stitching.* This interesting technique is often used in freehand embroidery to give texture and shading to a design. For a little variety try spark stitching with one color on the bobbin and another on top. By choosing the right colors, you can get an iridescent look to the stitch.

Corded Monograms

Stitching over a cord of pearl cotton or embroidery floss creates a lovely raised look to this satin-stitched monogram. It is a good choice for towels, linens, and other firmly woven fabrics.

Wind a bobbin with darning thread, available through your local sewing machine dealer. Darning thread, usually available in white or black only, is finer than ordinary embroidery thread so you do not constantly have to re-wind bobbins. Since the bobbin thread will probably be a different color than the top thread, *the upper tension must be loosened* so the stitches will lock *under* the work on the wrong side. This technique is for zigzag and reverse-action machines.

Step 1: Couching

Stitch: . . . . Zigzag stitch
Foot: . . . . Embroidery foot
Stitch length: . . 1 to 2mm. or 15 to 20 stitches per inch
Stitch width: . . 2mm.

1. Trace monogram on a piece of tissue paper. (If you do not like the monogram you have de-signed, patterns are usually avail-able at fabric stores or news-stands.) Place paper over the area you wish to monogram. If you are monogramming on terry cloth, paper under the stitching keeps the loops of the terry from poking through the stitches. Put fabric, with tissue pattern, in

your embroidery hoop, stretched drum tight.

2. Place a piece of pearl cotton or embroidery floss under the presser foot and couch it down, following the monogram outline with the zigzag stitch previously described (figure 8-12).

3. Remove the presser foot from the machine and either drop the feed dog to the "down" position or cover them with the darning plate.

Step 2: Practice Exercise (Spaghetti Embroidery)

Before starting the monogram, you may want to practice moving a fabric scrap, stretched in a hoop, under the needle. Set your machine as described below.

Stitch: . . . . Zigzag stitch
Foot: . . . . None
Stitch length: . . 0mm. or drop feed dog or cover feed with darning plate
Stitch width: . . 2mm., 3mm., 4mm.

Loosen upper tension.

1. With test fabric stretched drum tight in an embroidery hoop, place work under the nee-dle and lower the presser bar.

2. Holding the upper thread end in your left hand, turn the flywheel with your right, so the needle picks up the bobbin thread. Bring bobbin thread through the fabric and take a couple of locking stitches. Cut

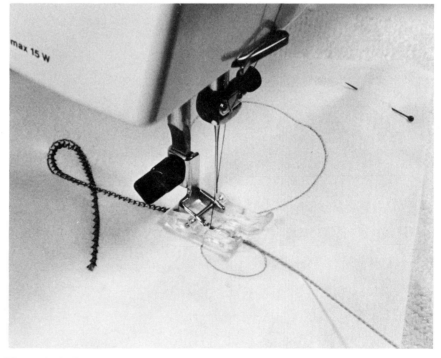

Figure 8-12 Cord monogram (step 1).

109

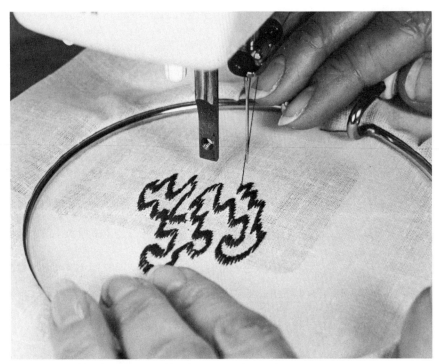

Figure 8-13 Freehand embroidery exercise (step 2).

thread ends off at the fabric so they will not get caught in the work.

3. While the needle is stitching, practice moving the fabric under the needle as if you were moving a piece of paper under a stationary pen. By stitching quickly and moving your hands slowly, you will get a beautiful satin stitch (figure 8-13). *Hint:* Keep the work in front of you, moving it from side to side without pivoting the hoop at a curve. This gives the proper taper to a freehand satin stitch. Now you are ready to monogram on the real thing.

Step 3: Final Stitching

1. With work prepared as described in Steps 1, and machine set as described in Step 2, stitch over the freehand monogram three times; so the first stitching is done with a narrow 2mm. stitch width.

2. Stitching quickly and moving your hands slowly, begin monogramming over tissue pattern and fabric so the needle zigzags over the corded monogram. Rip tissue paper off the work.

3. Stitch over the monogram a second time with a 3mm. stitch width, then a third time with a 4mm. stitch width. This gives a three-dimensional look to the monogram found on ready-to-wear monograms (figure 8-14). Trim away loose threads close to the fabric.

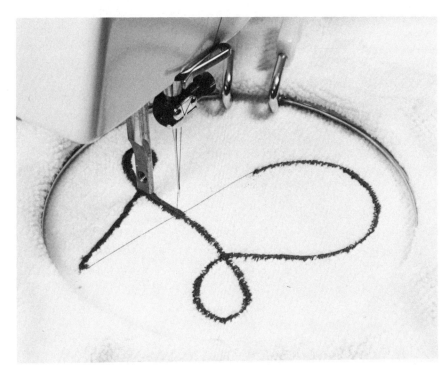

Figure 8-14 Monogram (step 3).

Tapered Monograms

Tapered monogramming is just another way to personalize linens and other gift items.

The monogram is made with the embroidery foot. Using the embroidery foot is important, because the grooved section under it allows the stitches to be sewn without flattening them into the fabric. Tapered monogramming is done only on zigzag and reverse-action machines.

Zigzag Sewing Machine

Step 1

Stitch: . . . . Zigzag stitch
Foot: . . . . Embroidery foot
Stitch length: . . 2mm. or 15 stitches per inch
Stitch width: . . 2mm.

1. Trace the monogram on the fabric or a piece of tissue paper. Tape or pin the paper to your fabric.

2. Place a piece of pearl cotton or embroidery floss under the foot and couch it down with the zigzag stitch previously described, stitching over paper and fabric following the outline of the monogram. *Hint:* For extra control, you may find it is easier to work with the fabric stretched drum tight in an embroidery hoop.

3. Rip paper off of work.

Figure 8-15 Tapered monogram.

Step 2

Stitch: . . . . Satin stitch (zigzag stitch)
Foot: . . . . Embroidery foot
Stitch length: . . ½mm. or fine setting
Stitch width: . . 1mm. to 4mm. back to 1mm.

Loosen upper tension and thread bobbin with darning thread.

1. The easiest way to taper a satin stitch is to run the machine quickly while smoothly moving the stitch-width knob or lever from 1mm. to 4mm. then back to 1mm. as will be described. Practice this a few times, first on a fabric scrap with tissue pattern on top and stretched tautly in an embroidery hoop. *Hint:* If the stitches are puckering, place a piece of heavier paper or inter-facing *under* the work.

2. Using your fingers like a center point in a compass, begin sewing, pivoting the fabric where necessary to complete the monogram. Tapered monograms look the best when the beginning of the line starts out narrow, gets wider at the center, then tapers to nothing at the other end (figure 8-15).

Once you have mastered tapering a monogram with the satin stitch, you will be able to taper other stitches to create leaf and petal shapes.

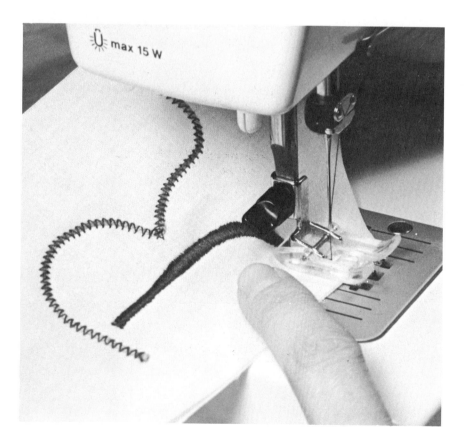

Reverse-Action Sewing Machine

Monograms made using reverse-action stitches and a presser foot can also be a combination of block and tapered styles. A block monogram is a letter with straight, rather than curved, lines. The stitch is the same width throughout each line in the letter (figure 8-16).

1. Transfer the monogram pattern to the background fabric, using a transfer pen or pencil (available at needlework shops), or by outlining the shape with basting stitches in a color matching the background fabric (page 40). The following reverse-action stitches look the best for tapered and/or block monograms:

Stitch suggestions: Feather, picot, smocking, or daisy stitch

Foot: . . . . Embroidery foot
Stitch length: . . Stretch-stitch or
cam setting
Stitch width: . . 3 to 4mm.

2. Study the examples shown for monogram ideas. A variety of stitches has been used (figure 8-16). *Hint:* If the stitches are puckering, place a piece of paper or interfacing under the work.

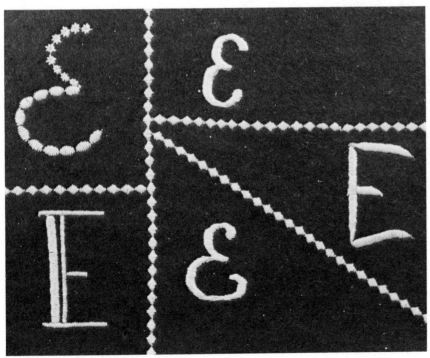

Figure 8-16 Decorative monograms.

MACHINE-EMBROIDERY TECHNIQUES

Most machine embroidery requires the use of the zigzag stitch. Therefore, techniques discussed in this section apply to zigzag and reverse-action sewing machines only.

Machine embroidery is done by using built-in or cam-operated stitches with an embroidery presser foot, or freehand, by moving the fabric under a moving needle without using a presser foot. The most suitable fabrics, threads, needles, and other necessary supplies for machine embroidery are discussed on pages 27–36. To be an expert at machine embroidery, tools are very important. Double-check to see if your machine has been cleaned and oiled, (page 137) and if there is a new needle in place before trying cutwork, freehand fill-in embroidery, reverse-machine embroidery, or other exciting techniques explained on the following pages.

Cutwork

Cutwork is one of the oldest embroidery forms and looks much more difficult than it really is. A basic rule to remember is any area that has been cut away must be reinforced so the stitching will not pull away from the fabric after some use. Cutwork is a combination of both presser-foot controlled and freehand embroidery. To illustrate how these techniques are done, we will create a beautiful embroidered flower.

Step 1: Outlining

Stitch: . . . . Zigzag stitch
Foot: . . . . Embroidery foot
Stitch length: . . 1 to 2mm. or 15
to 20 stitches per
inch
Stitch width: . . 2 to 3mm.

   1. Transfer the shape to be cut away onto a piece of firmly woven fabric. Stretch work drum tight in an embroidery hoop.
   2. Place a piece of pearl cotton or embroidery floss under the foot and couch it down with the zigzag stitch previously described, following the outline of the area to be cut away (figure 8-17).
   3. Using a sharp pair of embroidery scissors, trim away the fabric up to the stitches, inside the stitched area.

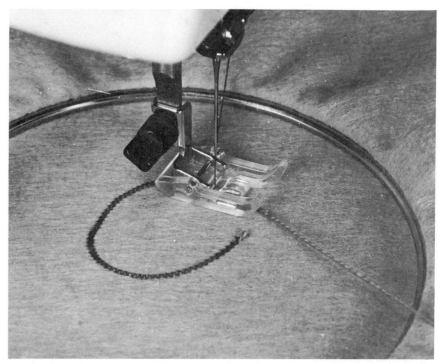

Figure 8-17 Couch over pearl cotton (step 1).

Step 2: Overcasting

Stitch: . . . . Satin stitch
(zigzag stitch)
Foot: . . . . Embroidery foot
Stitch length: . . ½mm. or fine
setting
Stitch width: . . 4mm.

Loosen upper tension.

   1. Place the work under the foot so the needle catches the fabric on one side and swings off the edge into the cutaway area on the other, to stitch over the couching (figure 8-18).

Figure 8-18 Overcast cutwork (step 2).

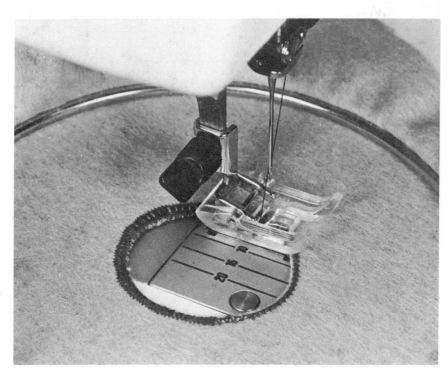

Step 3: Webbing Effects

Stitch: . . . . Straight stitch
Foot: . . . . None
Stitch length: . . 0mm., drop feed
    dog or cover
    feed with darning
    plate
Stitch width: . . 0mm.

1. Place the work, stretched drum tight in a hoop, under the needle at the outside edge of the stitching. Lower the presser bar. Using the cutwork as a frame for the webbing, turn the flywheel by hand, bringing the bobbin thread up through the fabric.

2. Take a couple of locking stitches and cut thread ends off at the fabric.

3. Begin stitching at one side of the cutwork frame and sew to the other, keeping stitches firm over the hole. Begin weaving a web across the cutwork hole, crossing the stitches where desired. Create an abstract design (figure 8-19) or a realistic one, as shown in the cutwork tennis racket pictured in figure 8-20.

To finish the design, use the zigzag stitch and create beautiful freehand embroidery as follows.

Freehand Machine Embroidery

Like freehand monogramming, freehand embroidery is one of the easiest sewing techniques to learn because it is nothing more than organized darning. Remember to *relax*, have a good time with it, and you will have a finished design you can be proud of, often in less than an hour. It can only be done on zigzag and reverse-action machines.

Step 1: Outlining

Stitch: . . . . Zigzag stitch
Foot: . . . . None
Stitch length: . . 0mm., drop feed
    dog or cover
    feed with darning
    plate
Stitch width: . . 2 to 4mm.

Loosen upper tension.

1. Transfer the embroidery pattern to the background fabric, using a transfer pen or pencil (available at needlework shops), or by outlining the shape with basting stitches in a color matching the background fabric.

2. Using the cutwork hole with webbing made in the previous section as the center of a flower, start embroidery at the outside edge of cutwork. Turn the flywheel by hand, bringing the bob-

Figure 8-19 Webbing (step 3).

Figure 8-20 Webbed tennis racket.

114

bin thread through the fabric.

3. Take a couple of locking stitches and cut thread ends at the fabric.

4. Begin stitching quickly, while slowly moving the fabric to the left, creating one side of the flower petal. The angle at which you hold the hoop creates the proper taper to the stitch. *Hint:* The slower you move the fabric while stitching, the better the satin stitch looks.

5. Back at the center of the cutwork hole, pivot the work slightly, then make a second flower petal, as before. Continue making petals until the design is complete (figure 8-21).

Step 2: Freehand Straight Stitch for Veins and Seeds

Stitch: . . . . Straight stitch
Foot: . . . . None
Stitch length: . . 0mm., drop feed dog or cover feed with darning plate
Stitch width: . . 0mm.

1. Move the stitch width to "0". Create the veins on the petals and seeds in the center of the flower by moving the design under the needle, as if you were moving a piece of paper under a stationary pen.

For more interest, sign your work using this technique (figure 8-22). After mastering the techniques already described, you will be able to machine embroider almost anything. Just use your imagination.

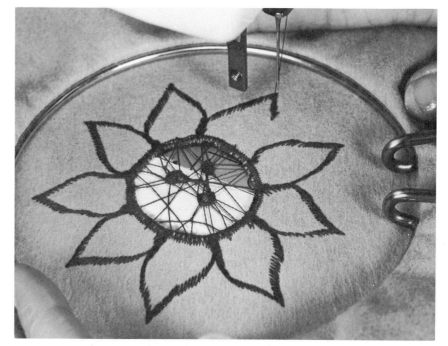

Figure 8-21 Freehand outlining (step 1).

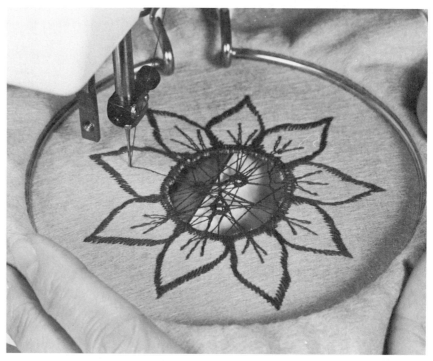

Figure 8-22 Veins and seeds (step 2).

Freehand Fill-In Embroidery

As the name implies, this technique is used to fill in a solid area with stitching.

Stitch: . . . . Zigzag stitch
Foot: . . . . None
Stitch length: . . 0mm., drop feed dog or cover feed with darning plate
Stitch width: . . 2 to 4mm.—the larger the area, the wider the stitch.

Loosen upper tension and thread bobbin with darning thread.

1. Transfer design on background fabric using transfer pen or pencil (available at needlework shops) or by outlining the shape with basting stitches in a color matching the background fabric. You can also use a preprinted design from a hand embroidery kit. Study the directional stitching on the pictured instructions. This will be helpful in planning the directional stitching sewn by machine. *Hint:* If you want embroidery on a heavy or bulky garment, make an embroidery appliqué. Transfer the design onto a piece of paper, then place paper under a woven see-through fabric, like organza, for a visible outline (figure 8-23). Embroider design as described below, then cut it out and appliqué the embroidered design to the background fabric.

2. Place the work, stretched drum tight in a hoop, under the needle. Lower the presser bar. Turn the flywheel by hand, bringing the bobbin thread up through the fabric. Sew a couple of locking stitches, then cut thread ends off at the fabric.

3. Using the appropriate settings on your machine, lightly outline the design in the direction the stitches are going to be sewn. For example, if the design is an animal, the directional stitching is going to be sewn in the direction the fur grows.

4. After outlining, fill the area in with a smooth, side-to-side motion for a satiny look to the work (figure 8-23). *Do not* fill in a design by moving the work up and down. The stitching will look rough, resulting in undesirable columns of stitching. Instead, work from the middle of the design outward, section by section.

5. When changing upper thread colors, simply cut upper thread at the fabric. Thread the machine with another color and start embroidery. No need to cut the bobbin thread because you are using the same bobbin for all embroidery. *Hint:* For truly invisible bobbin thread, wind it with clear nylon monofilament thread.

Reverse Machine Embroidery

Even though I was a home economics major in college, I never learned crewel embroidery—not for lack of interest, but for the lack of time. You can imagine how delighted I was when I found out I could create beautiful embroidery, easily, by machine.

Figure 8-23 Zigzag fill-in.

Reverse machine embroidery emulates hand embroidery more than any other form of machine embroidery. Pearl cotton or embroidery floss is wound on a bobbin, and the design is sewn with the right side of the fabric upside-down. It can be used to decorate children's clothing, and to cover hemlines in corduroy or denim that will not press out. It can also add a special touch to household and/or gift items. By combining all aspects of machine embroidery with reverse-embroidery, a design is more interesting and takes practically no time to complete. Before trying reverse machine embroidery, however, investigate the bobbin system on your machine, because some machines are *not* equipped to work with pearl cotton or embroidery floss in the bobbin.

To use pearl cotton or embroidery floss in the bobbin, you must either have a removable bobbin case or a top-loading bobbin with a tension by-pass hole in the race mechanism (figure 8-9, page 107). If you have a removable bobbin case, I recommend you buy a second one for experimental tension adjustment.

First, wind a bobbin with desired color of pearl cotton or embroidery floss, by machine. Place the pearl cotton or floss in your lap and guide it on the bobbin evenly by hand, as the bobbin turns. If using floss on a skein, wind floss onto an empty spool, then wind the bobbin. *Do not overwind bobbin.*

Removable bobbin cases: Some bobbin cases have a hole in the top, or just to one side, where

pearl cotton or floss can be threaded, and the bobbin tension by-passed (figure 8-9, page 107). If you do not have the tension by-pass hole, thread bobbin case with pearl cotton or floss through normal bobbin tension. Begin loosening the tension screw on the bobbin case, until the pearl cotton or floss pulls smoothly through the tension. After threading bobbin case, place it in the machine and bring the bobbin thread up. Upper thread color should match pearl cotton or floss.

Top-loading bobbins with tension by-pass hole: Using a bobbin filled with pearl cotton or embroidery floss, thread floss through the tension by-pass hole as illustrated (figure 8-9, page 107). Upper thread color should match pearl cotton or floss. *Note:* The technique for reverse ma-

chine embroidery is the same for both zigzag and reverse-action sewing machines as described— only the stitches differ.

Zigzag Sewing Machine

Stitch Suggestions: Straight, zigzag, blind hem, stretch blind hem, ball, or diamond stitch

Foot: . . . . Embroidery foot
Stitch length: . . ¾mm. or fine
               setting
Stitch width: . . 4mm.

Reverse-Action Sewing Machine

Stitch Suggestions: Feather, smocking, cross stitch, wave stitch, or any other tracery design

Foot: . . . . Embroidery foot
Stitch length: . . Stretch-stitch or
               cam setting
Stitch width: . . 4mm.

Figure 8-24 Reverse embroidery.

Figure 8-25 Reverse embroidery.

1. Test for desired stitch on scrap piece of background fabric.

2. Transfer the design to the *wrong* side of the background fabric.

3. If using a lightweight fabric, transfer the design onto a piece of paper or interfacing, and place that over the wrong side of the fabric. Stitch over the paper or interfacing and your fabric. This extra support prevents unnecessary puckering.

4. Follow the lines on the transferred design with desired stitch for an exciting pillow cover, table runner, or wall hanging (figure 8-24, 25). *Hint:* If you are planning to use several colors in the bobbin, use clear nylon monofilament thread on top. This way, you will not have to change the upper thread for different colored bobbins. To use this type of thread successfully, place a fat, plastic drinking straw, the kind you get at fast food restaurants, over the spool pin. Then put the spool of monofilament thread over the straw on the spool pin. This way, the thread will not spill off the spool or backlash around the spool pin and break.

MACHINE-EMBROIDERED EDGE FINISHES

There are many ways to finish edges on table linens, scarves, shawls, and shirt hems that save a lot of time when done by machine. In every case, cut the project longer or wider than you need it because the stitching is done at the hemline and excess fabric trimmed off afterward. The following edge finishes are only possible on zigzag and reverse-action machines.

Corded Satin-Stitch Edge Finish

One of the most common ways to finish a raw edge is with a corded satin stitch.

Step 1

Stitch: . . . . Zigzag stitch
Foot: . . . . Embroidery foot
Stitch length:. . 2mm. or 15 stitches per inch
Stitch width: . . 2 to 3mm. (a 2mm. width is used for a narrow finished edge, a 3mm. width is used for a wider finished edge).

Top and bobbin threaded with matching colors.

1. Under the presser foot on the hemline, place two to four strands of pearl cotton or floss in the same or similar color as the top and bobbin thread. Stitch pearl cotton or floss around the edge of the project with the zig-zag stitch previously described (figure 8-26).

2. Using a pair of sharp embroidery scissors, trim excess fabric off close to the stitching, being careful not to cut threads.

Step 2

Stitch: . . . . Satin stitch (zigzag stitch)
Foot: . . . . Embroidery foot
Stitch length:. . ½ to ¾mm. or fine setting
Stitch width: . . 3 to 4mm.

1. Using a slightly wider satin stitch, place the corded edge under the presser foot so the needle swings into corded edge on the left and the stitch locks off the edge on the right.

2. When you get to a corner, pivot work slightly when the needle is on the inside of the work. Stitches should fan out from the corner for a professional finish.

3. Complete stitching and tie off thread ends.

Step 3

Stitch: . . . . Zigzag stitch
Foot: . . . . Embroidery foot
Stitch length:. . 2mm. or 15 stitches per inch
Stitch width: . . 2mm.

1. Using a narrow zigzag stitch as described, place a piece of pearl cotton or embroidery floss under the presser foot and couch it down on either side of the satin stitch (figure 8-27).

Figure 8-26 Edge finish (step 1).

Figure 8-27 Edge finish (step 3).

Decorative Stitches for Edge Finishes

Use your built-in and cam stitches for exceptional decorative embroidered edge finishes for your projects.

Eyelash Edge Finish

Stitch: .... Stretch blind-hem stitch
Foot: .... Embroidery foot
Stitch length: .. ½mm. or fine setting
Stitch width: .. 4mm.

1. Cut project longer and wider than you need it.
2. On the hemline, place one strand of pearl cotton under the *right* side of the embroidery presser foot.
3. Using the stretch-blind-hem stitch previously described, stitch around the hemline of the project, over the pearl cotton. At the corner, pivot the work slightly when the needle makes the long stitch in the left. Stitches should fan out from the corner for a professional finish.
4. Using a pair of sharp embroidery scissors, trim excess fabric close to the stitching line, being careful not to cut the stitches (figure 8-28). *Hint:* For a firmer edge, you may want to satin stitch over eyelash edge with a 2mm.-wide satin stitch. Guide work so the needle bites into the fabric on the left and swings off finished edge on the right.

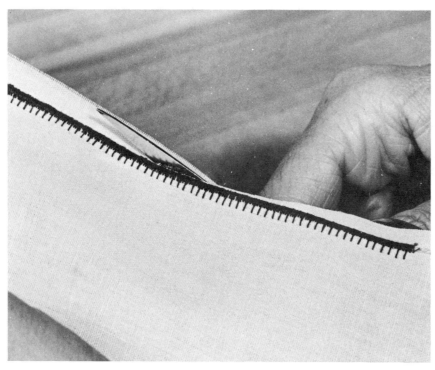

Figure 8-28 Stretch blind-hem edge finish.

120

Scallop Edge Finish

Stitch: . . . . Tracery scallop
                          stitch
Foot: . . . . Embroidery foot
Stitch length: . . 1 to 2mm. or 15
                          to 20 stitches per
                          inch
Stitch width: . . 4mm.

Step 1

1. Test the length of the tracery scallop stitch on a fabric scrap.

2. On the hemline, begin stitching scallops, being careful not to distort the stitch pattern at the corners by pushing or pulling the fabric.

3. Using a pair of sharp embroidery scissors, trim excess fabric up to the stitching line.

Step 2

Stitch: . . . . Satin stitch
                          (zigzag stitch)
Foot: . . . . Embroidery foot
Stitch length: . . ½mm. or fine
                          setting
Stitch width: . . 2 to 3mm.

1. Place the work under the presser foot so the needle bites into the fabric at the left and swings off the scallop-stitched edge at the right.

2. Carefully satin stitch the edge, using the tracery scallop as a guide. A perfect scallop is finished in no time (figure 8-29).

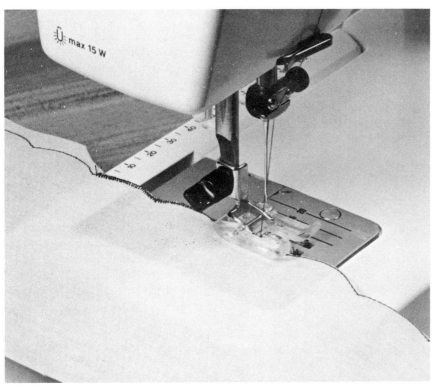

Figure 8-29 Satin-stitched scallop (step 2).

YARN EMBROIDERY

Until recently, no one realized that the sewing machine was capable of working with yarn similar to that used in beautiful, but time-consuming, crewel embroidery done by hand. Different types of yarns are used to create stitches anyone can master, and yarn embroidery can be done on all three types of machines—straight-stitch, zigzag, and reverse-action. When choosing a design, however, keep it large and simple. The center of the design must be made before the outer areas.

Preparation

No matter what yarn stitch you are creating by machine, the preparation is the same for all types of machines. Have the following supplies on hand: firmly woven fabric, embroidery hoop, tweezers, embroidery scissors, nylon monofilament thread, a variety of yarn. Transfer design on background fabric as described on page 100.

Machine Settings For All Yarn Embroidery Stitches

Stitch: . . . . Straight stitch
Foot: . . . . None
Stitch length: . . 0mm., drop feed
                          dog or cover
                          feed with darning
                          plate
Stitch width: . . 0mm.

1. Wind a bobbin with clear nylon monofilament thread, being careful not to overwind the bobbin. Thread bobbin case as you

would with regular sewing thread.

2. The top thread must also be clear nylon monofilament thread. *Hint:* To prevent thread from spilling off the spool or backlashing around the spool pin, place a fat, plastic drinking straw, the kind you get at fast food restaurants, over the spool pin, then place the spool of thread over the straw.

3. Place the background fabric, stretched drum tight in a hoop, under the needle.

4. Lower the presser bar and turn the flywheel by hand, bringing the bobbin thread up through the fabric. Sew a couple of locking stitches and cut thread ends off at the fabric. Remember that the center of a design must be made first. For this design example, yarn loops are a good place to begin.

Yarn Loops

This is good for flower centers or fur on animals. Prepare design and machine as explained earlier.

1. Place yarn end at the inside of the design to begin yarn loops.

2. Sew a few locking stitches to anchor the yarn end and cut it close to the fabric so it will not interfere with the rest of the embroidery.

3. Hold the embroidery hoop and yarn with your left hand.

4. Using a pair of long tweezers held in your right hand, pull a loop the desired length and stitch at the base of loop between the tweezers and your left hand (figure 8-30).

5. Pull a second loop and anchor it as before, next to the first. Continue till desired area is covered with loops. After loops are made, you can leave them "loopy" or cut them for a rougher texture.

Satin Stitch

This is recommended for flower petals and leaves. Prepare design and machine as explained on page 121.

1. Place yarn end at the edge of the outline. Sew a couple of locking stitches to anchor the yarn, and cut yarn off close to the fabric so it will not interfere with the rest of the embroidery.

2. Hold the work in the hoop with your right hand and the yarn in your left. Move the work so the machine needle takes a few straight stitches to the other side of the design on background fabric, being careful *not* to sew through the yarn every time you walk the needle across the design. The next yarn satin stitch will cover the machine stitching. With your left hand, draw the yarn taut across the design and anchor it with a few straight stitches at the design outline (figure 8-31).

3. Again, move the work with your right hand while holding the yarn in your left. Let the needle travel to the other side of the outline without sewing through the yarn. Bring the yarn to the outline and anchor it with a few

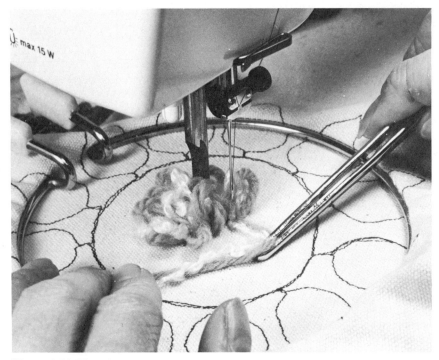

Figure 8-30 Yarn loops.

straight stitches. Be sure that one length of yarn is next to the other for a smooth satin stitch (figure 8-31).

4. Continue the process until the design is complete. To anchor satin stitch, take a few locking stitches in place over yarn; cut yarn off at the fabric.

5. To create veins in flower petals or leaves, move the satin-stitched design under the needle as it is stitching in the desired pattern. The stitching gives a three-dimensional look to the embroidery.

Chain Stitch

This is an appropriate stitch for outlining, branches, and stems. Prepare design and machine as explained on page 121.

1. Cut two strands of yarn the same length.

2. Place the double strand of yarn on design line so the middle of the strands are anchored to the background fabric. Sew a few locking stitches.

3. With one length of yarn in one hand and the other length in the other hand, twist yarn strands and sew a few locking stitches down one of the twisted yarn channels.

4. Continue this process until you have the chain stitch the desired length (figure 8-32). Clip yarn ends off at the fabric, or leave yarn ends free to create a fringe effect.

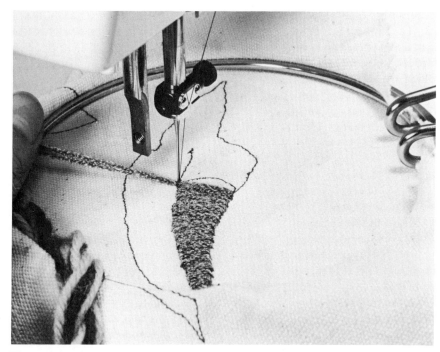

Figure 8-31 Yarn satin stitch.

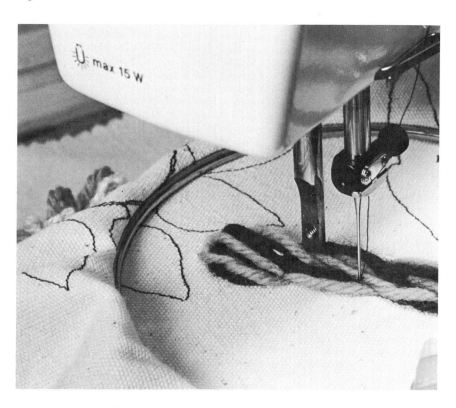

Figure 8-32 Yarn chain stitch.

TWIN-NEEDLE SEWING

Learning how to use twin needles was one of my favorite sewing discoveries. Before I knew better, I thought twin needles were used only for decorative sewing, but they work well for quick hemming, sewing permanent creases in slacks, and for making decorative pin tucks. You can even create a cable stitch that looks like it was knitted or woven into the fabric.

A twin needle has two needles connected to one shaft, as pictured on page 31. In every case, the needle must be inserted with the flat side to the back of the machine. Twin needles vary in size and are identified by a number indicating the distance between the needles and the needle size. For example, a twin needle identified by the numbers 2.0/70 means that the needles are 2mm. apart and are a European size 70 (American size 10–11). Twin needles are also available through your local sewing machine dealer in the following sizes: 2.7/80, 3.0/90, and 4.0/100. Finer needles are used on lightweight fabrics; heavier needles are used on heavier fabrics.

Although the twin needle works on most zigzag and reverse-action machines, it will only work on machines with top- or front-loading bobbins. If you have a question about this, consult your sewing machine instruction book or call your local dealer.

Figure 8-33 Pin tucks.

Upper-threading requires two spools of thread. The machine is threaded normally, but threads are separated at the upper tension and at the thread guide above and before the needles. Machine settings vary with the stitch selection, but remember: when setting a stitch width, *do not* use a full 4mm. stitch width, because the needles might swing too wide, hit the presser foot, and break.

In twin-needle sewing, one bobbin thread is shared by the two top threads. This makes the bobbin thread look like a zigzag stitch on the wrong side of the work, but what it does is pull the two upper threads together, creating a tuck.

Twin-Needle Pin Tucking

For straight and even pin tucks, buy a pin-tucking foot as pictured on page 22. This foot has channels under it that allow tucks to be sewn at an even distance apart and gives a crisp edge to each tuck. Generally, you do not have to add extra fabric to your pattern to make these tucks, unless you plan to make more than ten. In this case, make the tucks in your fabric *before* you cut out the pattern piece.

Stitch: .... Straight stitch
Foot: .... Pin-tucking foot
Stitch length:.. 2 to 3mm. or 10
                to 15 stitches per
                inch
Stitch width: .. 0mm.

For crisper tucks, tighten the upper tension slightly.

1. Place a single layer of fabric under the foot, right side up.
2. Begin sewing. The pin tuck is pulled up between the two rows of stitching.
3. Sew the second row of pin-tucking, next to the first, guiding the first tuck down one of the channels in the pin-tucking foot. Continue sewing row after row of pin tucks for desired effect (figure 8-33). *Hint:* You may use one row of pin-tucking to give a crisper crease in a pair of slacks, or to better define the edge of a pleat.

Twin-Needle Shadow Work

Shadow work is created by the bobbin thread and fabric showing through transparent fabric, giving a darker, traced look to the stitch. Try shadow work on curtain hems and sheer, dressy clothes (figure 8-34).

Zigzag Sewing Machine

Stitch Suggestions: Straight, zigzag, multiple-zigzag, or tracery scallop stitch

Foot: . . . . Zigzag or embroidery foot
Stitch length:. . 2 to 3mm. or 10 to 15 stitches per inch
Stitch width: . . 2 to 2½mm.

Figure 8-34 Shadow work.

Reverse-Action Sewing Machine

Stitch Suggestions: Wave, leaf, or running daisy stitch

Foot: . . . . Zigzag or embroidery foot
Stitch length: . . Stretch-stitch or cam setting
Stitch width: . . 2 to 2½mm.

1. Loosen or by-pass bobbin tension (figure 8-9, page 107).
2. Fold hem up desired amount and press.
3. Place hem under presser foot so the foot rests on a double layer of fabric.
4. Stitch hem (figure 8-35). Trim raw edge close to the stitching line.

5. For shadow work on other garment areas, trace design on right side of sheer fabric. Place another, larger, layer of sheer fabric underneath top layer and stitch around the design.
6. Trim excess fabric from underneath, up to the stitching line. The combination of the second layer of fabric and the bobbin thread of the twin needle topstitch, creates the "shadow" effect on sheer fabrics.

Twin-Needle Cable Stitch

A machine cable design is made easily with a variety of stitches. Use them alone, or in combination with each other.

You can make cables on light-weight to medium-weight knits and wovens.

This technique gives interest down the center front, back, or sleeve of a knit sweater. It is easy to do and saves you hunting for ribbing or trim to make the project unique.

Zigzag Sewing Machine

Stitch Suggestions: Multiple-zig-zag or scallop stitch

Foot: . . . . Embroidery foot
Stitch length: . . 3mm. or 10 stitches per inch
Stitch width: . . 2 to 2½mm.

Reverse-Action Sewing Machine

Stitch Suggestions: Wave, Greek key, or leaf stitch

Foot: . . . . Embroidery foot
Stitch length: . . Stretch-stitch or cam setting
Stitch width: . . 2 to 2½mm.

Thread a fine or small-size twin needle with thread that matches your fashion fabric.

1. With a transfer pen or pencil, mark cable placement on your fabric.
2. Place single layer of fabric under presser foot and sew the first row of stitching.
3. Sew the second and third rows on either side of the first, as shown in the illustration.
4. If a wider cable is desired, sew additional rows of twin-needle cable stitching next to each other (figure 8-36).

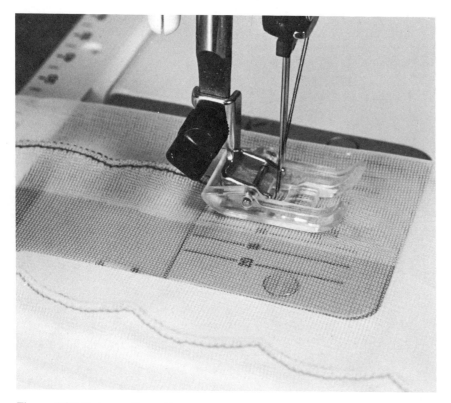

Figure 8-35 Twin-needle scallop.

GATHERING

The fashionable look these days is feminine, and with it comes ruffles and gathers. Sometimes, however, these special touches can be difficult.

Most pattern instructions tell you to use two rows of long, basting stitches, then pull up on the threads. If you are like me, the basting stitches break before you are finished adjusting the gathers. The following are some ideas that make gathering easier, will save you time, and will prevent the threads from breaking while gathers are being adjusted.

Straight-Stitch Sewing Machine

Method 1

Stitch: . . . . Straight stitch
Foot: . . . . Gathering foot
Stitch length:. . 2 to 4mm. or 6 to 15 stitches per inch (the more gathering desired, the longer the stitch)

1. Place work under the gathering foot.
2. Begin sewing. The foot makes the fabric gather automatically. *Note:* Test the amount of gathering on a fabric scrap so you can figure out how much the work will pull up. This system of gathering is great, but you cannot adjust gathers after the stitching is completed (figure 8-37).

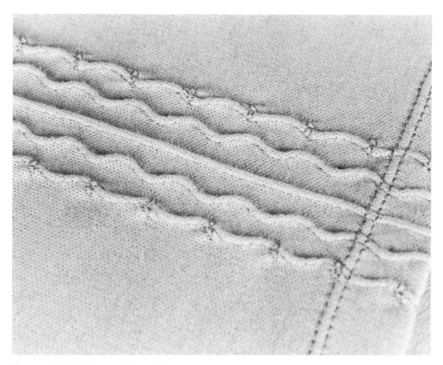

Figure 8-36 Twin-needle cable.

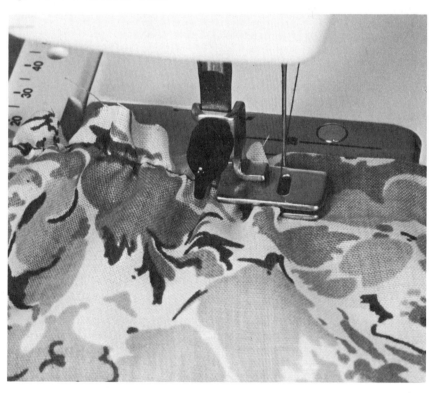

Figure 8-37 Gathering foot (method 1).

127

Figure 8-38 Double-thread gathering (method 2).

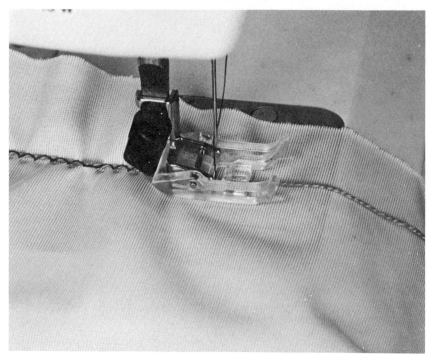

Figure 8-39 Zigzagging over cord.

Method 2

Stitch: . . . . Straight stitch
Foot: . . . . Straight-stitch
                    foot
Stitch length: . . 3 to 4mm. or 6
                    to 10 stitches per
                    inch (the heavier
                    the fabric, the
                    longer the stitch)

1. Thread the machine needle with topstitching thread or use two threads through one needle.

2. Loosen upper tension.

3. Sew one or two rows of basting stitches in the seam allowance.

4. Remove the work from the machine and pull the heavier upper thread, adjusting gathers as you go. By using a heavier upper thread, the stress of the fabric will not break the gathering stitches (figure 8-38).

Zigzag and Reverse-Action Sewing Machine

Stitch: . . . . Zigzag stitch
Foot: . . . . Zigzag or
                    embroidery foot
Stitch length: . . 2 to 4mm. or 6
                    to 15 stitches per
                    inch (the heavier
                    the fabric, the
                    longer the stitch)
Stitch width: . . 2 to 3mm.

1. Place wrong side of fabric under presser foot with needle ½-inch (1.3cm.) from raw edge.

2. Place a strand of pearl-cotton cording or embroidery floss under the presser foot. *Hint:* If you want a stretchy gather, sew over a piece of elastic thread.

3. Zigzag *over* pearl cotton to

create a thread casing for cording to slide through (figure 8-39). *Note:* The needle must *not* stitch through the cording.

4. Hold pearl cotton on one end and pull fabric with the other hand to create and adjust gathers. Knot or anchor cording ends so gathers do not shift when pinning garment together (figure 8-40).

BELT LOOPS

Crocheted belt loops are easy to make by hand but are much faster by machine.

The resulting cord is fine enough to thread on a large eyed needle and can be sewn into the waistline seam for belt carriers.

Zigzag and Reverse-Action Sewing Machines

Stitch: . . . . Zigzag stitch
Foot: . . . . Embroidery foot
Stitch length: . . ½ to ¾mm. or fine setting
Stitch width: . . 4mm.

1. Knot four to six strands of sewing thread or two strands of pearl cotton at one end.
2. Place the multiple strand under the presser foot. Hold threads or pearl cotton strands with one hand in front and one hand in back of the foot.
3. Hold the top and bobbin threads in the hand behind the machine and begin sewing. The zigzag stitches will cover the strands of thread or pearl cotton.
4. Move the multiple strands of thread or pearl cotton slowly under the presser foot while sewing (figure 8-41).

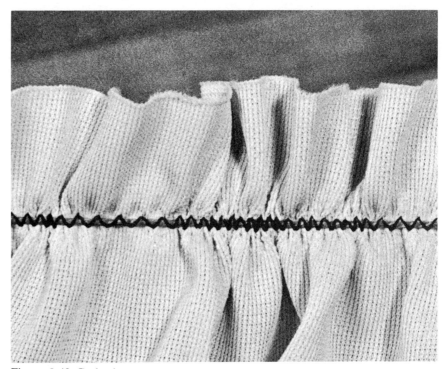

Figure 8-40 Gathering.

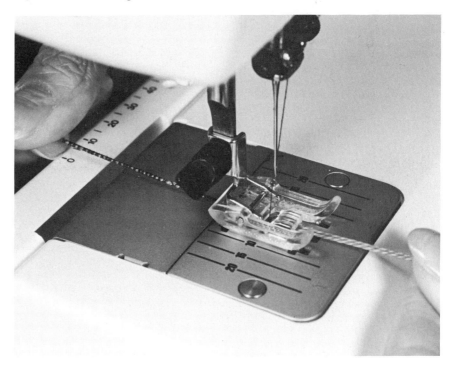

Figure 8-41 Belt loops.

SPAGHETTI STRAPS

Zigzag and Reverse-Action
Sewing Machines

Stitch: . . . . Zigzag stitch
Foot: . . . . Embroidery foot
Stitch length: . . 3 to 4mm. or 6
    to 10 stitches per
    inch
Stitch width: . . 4mm.

1. Cut a ¾-inch (2cm.) wide strip of nylon tricot, or any single knit or jersey on the crosswise grain.

2. Stretch the fabric strip so the edges curl in, forming a long tube.

3. Place the tube under the presser foot, stretching it with one hand in front and one hand in back of the foot.

4. Begin sewing with the zigzag stitch, taking care that the stitch clears the fabric on both sides (figure 8-42). *Hint:* If the needle hits the fabric, cut a narrower strip.

In no time, the strap is sewn without having to turn it the old-fashioned way.

SMOCKING

Smocking has traditionally been done by hand and is a craft by itself. Smocking can also be done by machine on most lightweight to medium-weight woven or knit fabrics. Machine smocking is done with elastic thread in the bobbin, using some of the decorative stitches.

Since the elastic thread is responsible for pulling up the fabric to create the smocking, the success or failure of machine smocking depends on the type of elastic thread you use. The best kind is made in Switzerland, marketed under the name *Gold-Zack,* and is available through your local sewing machine dealer. This thread has a thick, rubber core and is covered with a 100 percent cotton casing. If you cannot find this type of elastic thread, look for some that is at least 60 percent cotton. The nylon-covered elastic thread often loses its stretch before it is sewn in the garment.

For sewing machines with the bobbin winder on the exterior, hold the spool of elastic thread on your lap and guide thread smoothly by hand as the bobbin turns on bobbin winder. If your machine has a self-winding bobbin, wind the elastic thread on the bobbin by hand. In either case, *do not* stretch the elastic thread on the bobbin. After winding the bobbin, thread bobbin case as you would with any ordinary thread. One of the problems most people have with machine smocking is that only the first few rows work well. When you get to the third or fourth row, the fabric begins to pucker up, the stitching is not straight, and the tension begins to cause problems. All this can be eliminated by placing a strip of *paper adding-machine tape* under the work. It is the right weight of paper to keep the fabric flat when smocking. Afterward, it pulls off easily, and the

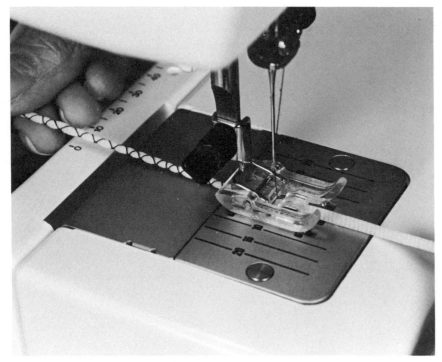

Figure 8-42 Spaghetti straps.

smocked area has even stitching lines and thread tensions.

Using the same fabric as your project, it is a good idea to test smock on a ten-inch (25cm.) strip of fabric. If, after smocking, the fabric measures 5 inches (12.5cm.), you will need twice as much fabric for smocked areas as for the rest of the project. In any case, if smocking is not called for on your pattern, you will need extra fabric.

Shirring

This is one of the easiest ways to smock and can be done on all types of sewing machines.

Straight-Stitch Sewing Machine

Stitch: .... Straight stitch
Foot: .... Straight-stitch foot
Stitch length:.. 2 to 4mm. or 6 to 15 stitches per inch

Zigzag Sewing Machine

Stitch: .... Zigzag stitch
Foot: .... Embroidery foot
Stitch length:.. 2 to 3mm. or 10 to 15 stitches per inch
Stitch width: .. 2 to 3mm.

Reverse-Action Sewing Machine

Stitch: .... Smocking stitch
Foot: .... Embroidery foot
Stitch length:.. Stretch-stitch or cam setting
Stitch width: .. 4mm.

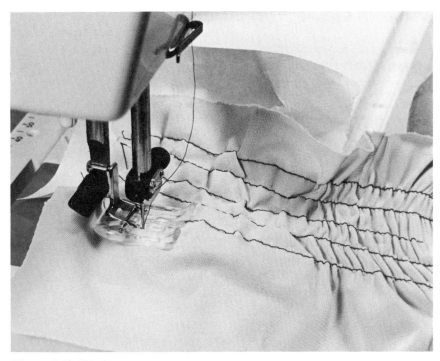

Figure 8-43 Shirring.

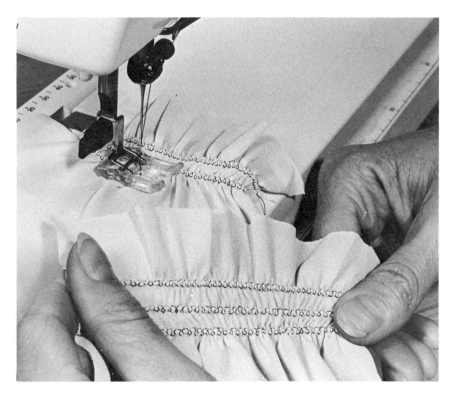

Figure 8-44 Smocking.

131

1. Thread bobbin with elastic thread.

2. Mark right side of fabric, where shirring is desired, with straight lines, using dressmaker's chalk or a transfer pen. Rows of shirring should be at least ½-inch (1.3cm.) apart.

3. To prevent fabric from shirring-up too soon, place a piece of adding-machine tape under the work for straight-stitch and zigzag machines only. *Note:* This is not necessary when using the smocking stitch on reverse-action machines, because you can get evenly shirred rows of stitching without it.

4. On a single layer of fabric, begin stitching the first row of shirring. Continue until the desired number of rows have been stitched, approximately a presser-foot width away from each other.

5. Rip the paper away from the fabric (figure 8-43, 8-44). When constructing the garment, be sure the elastic thread ends are anchored securely in the seams.

Rickrack Smocking

You can create the look of rickrack using pearl cotton in a color either matching or contrasting with your fabric. This technique creates a dramatic effect on the wrist area of sleeves, on childrens clothes, aprons, and other gift items.

Zigzag and Reverse-Action Sewing Machines

Stitch: . . . . Multiple-zigzag stitch
Foot: . . . . Embroidery foot
Stitch length: . . 1½mm. or 20 stitches per inch
Stitch width: . . 4mm.

1. Thread bobbin with elastic thread.

2. Mark area to be smocked. *Do not* use adding-machine tape under the work.

3. Place a single layer of fabric under the needle, right side up. Holding the top and bobbin thread in one hand, turn the flywheel so the needle is in the fabric and the presser foot is up. The needle should be centered in the middle of the multiple-zigzag stitch pattern when it goes into the fabric.

4. Place four strands of pearl cotton under the presser foot, putting two strands to one side of the needle and two strands to the other side of the needle. Lower the presser foot.

5. Begin sewing slowly. The elastic thread pulls the fabric so the strands of pearl cotton look like a piece of rickrack (figure 8-45). *Note:* Because the fabric is gathering as you are sewing, successive rows of rickrack smocking should be at least one inch (2.5cm.) apart.

Figure 8-45 Rickrack smocking.

Popcorn Smocking

Popcorn smocking is much faster than smocking by hand and is an interesting way to turn a solid fabric into something special. Try using other decorative stitches to create your own unique machine smock.

Zigzag Sewing Machine

Stitch: . . . . Multiple-zigzag
                 stitch
Foot: . . . . Embroidery foot
Stitch length: . . 1½ to 2mm. or
                 15 to 20 stitches
                 per inch
Stitch width: . . 4mm.

Reverse-Action Sewing Machine

Stitch: . . . . Running daisy
                 stitch
Foot: . . . . Embroidery foot
Stitch length: . . Stretch-stitch or
                 cam setting
Stitch width: . . 4mm.

Note: Before trying this technique on a garment, practice matching the design on a firmly woven piece of fabric *without* elastic thread in the bobbin. This way, you will not waste the elastic thread while you learn to match a stitch pattern.

1. Thread bobbin with elastic thread.
2. Place adding-machine tape under work. Mark the work to remember where the *body of the fabric* is. If you want to smock the wrist of a sleeve, the body of the fabric is where most of the fabric is from the end of the smocking up to the sleeve cap. Mark the body of the fabric with a

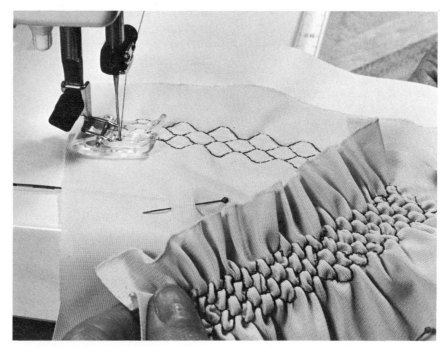

Figure 8-46 Popcorn smocking using a zigzag machine.

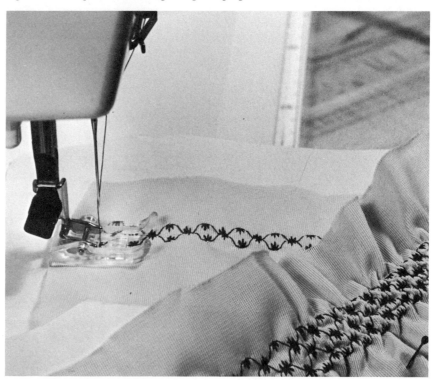

Figure 8-47 Popcorn smocking using a reverse-action machine.

133

pin as shown (figure 8-46). This will remind you which way to turn the fabric to match the stitch pattern.

3. Begin sewing on the right side of a single layer of fabric with one of the stitches described. When you get to the edge of the fabric, stop stitching when the needle is in the side of the stitch closest to the body of the fabric marked in Step 2. For example, if the body of the fabric is on your left, stop stitching when the needle is in the left side of the stitch (figure 8-46).

4. Lift the presser foot and pivot the fabric 180°.

5. Begin stitching slowly, matching up the design as you go. The points of the stitch must match to create the popcorn look (figure 8-47).

6. Rip paper off the back of the work. *Hint:* Paper is easier to remove if wet.

Twin-Needle Smocking

Twin-needle smocking is done *without* elastic thread and is a combination of hand and machine smocking.

Zigzag Sewing Machine

Stitch: . . . . Blind-hem stitch
Foot: . . . . Embroidery foot
Stitch length: . . 1½ to 2mm. or
                    15 to 20 stitches
                    per inch
Stitch width: . . 2mm.

Figure 8-48 Twin-needle smocking.

Reverse-Action Sewing Machine

Stitch: . . . . Couching stitch
Foot: . . . . Embroidery foot
Stitch length: . . Stretch-stitch or
                    cam setting
Stitch width: . . 2mm.

1. Thread twin needles and bobbin with thread matching your fabric (twin-needle threading, page 124).

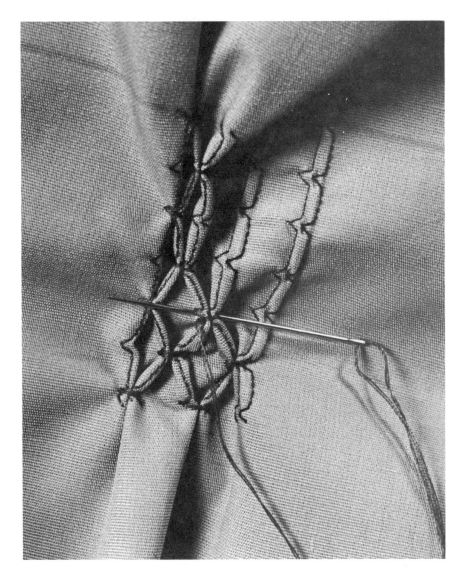

2. With dressmaker's chalk or transfer pen, mark a horizontal line across the top of the right side of a single layer of fabric. This will be the starting point of the stitching.

3. Using the appropriate stitch, begin sewing the first row of stitching across the fabric on the lengthwise grain. The stitch takes a few straight stitches, then a

small, zigzag stitch to one side. *Hint:* The small, zigzag stitch marks where the hand stitches will be sewn; so it is important to begin each row of stitching at the beginning of the stitch cycle.

4. No more than an inch (2.5cm.) apart, sew consecutive rows of parallel twin-needle tucks.

5. Tie off the machine stitching at ends. Thread hand-needle with a matching or contrasting thread, or a couple of strands of embroidery floss.

6. Using the small, zigzag stitches in the tucks as smocking points, begin smocking the rows (figure 8-48). Smocking goes quickly, and the hand stitches are even because the stitch automatically marks the fabric for you.

CIRCULAR SEWING

It is easy to sew perfect scallops on dust ruffles, lapels, or hemlines, or to stitch perfect circles as decorative touches on gift items. All you need is some tape and a thumbtack.

The following method is for zigzag and reverse-action machines. You can, however, use this method to make faced scallops on a straight-stitch machine (see Step 7).

Zigzag Sewing Machine

Stitch Suggestions: Zigzag, ball, or diamond stitch

Foot: . . . . Embroidery foot
Stitch length: . . ½mm. or fine setting
Stitch width: . . 4mm.

Reverse-Action Sewing Machine

Stitch Suggestions: Smocking or featherstitch

Foot: . . . . Embroidery foot
Stitch length: . . Stretch-stitch or cam setting
Stitch width: . . 4mm.

For a circular motif shown in figure 8-49:

1. Pierce a piece of tape with a thumbtack so the sticky side is against the inside of the tack and the point is up.

2. Place tack and tape on the bed of the machine with the point up. The point of the tack is the center of the circle; so place it directly to the right of the needle. The distance away from the needle should be the radius (half the diameter) of the circle. Pierce the fabric with the tack.

3. Use one of the suggested stitches and sew. The machine automatically turns the fabric around the tack point to make a perfect circle. *Note:* If you are using a soft fabric, stretch work drum tight in an embroidery hoop before stitching (figure 8-49).

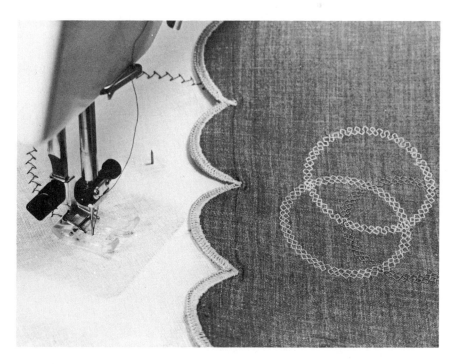

Figure 8-49 Circular sewing.

To make a scalloped edge as shown in figure 8-49:

1. Cut project, adding extra fabric to the edge where the scallops will be made. How much you add depends on how deep you wish the scallops to be.

2. With dressmaker's chalk or transfer pen, draw a line above the raw edge at least the width of the scallop plus ½-inch (1.3cm.).

3. Place tape and tack on the bed of the machine as described above. If the scallop is 3-inches (8cm.) wide, then put the tack 1½-inches (3.8cm.) to the right of the needle.

4. Place fabric on the tack at the line. Turn the fabric so the stitching starts on this line and begin sewing. The thumbtack works like the center point in a compass.

5. After sewing a half circle, at which point you will be back at the line, leave the needle in the work.

6. Lift the presser foot, take the fabric off the tack, and turn the work, using the needle as the pivot point. *Note:* If you want shallower scallops, draw a line ¼-to ½-inch (6mm. to 1.3cm.) down from, and parallel to the first. Tack will be positioned on the top-most line. You will only stitch up to the second line, then proceed as described.

7. Place the work back on the tack, further down on the line. Continue this process until the scallops are finished. *Hint:* A scalloped facing can be stitched on at the same time the scallops are being sewn, by placing two pieces of fabric with right sides together, and following the instructions above. Use a straight stitch, trim seam, clip to inner points of scallop, and turn the facing to the inside. Press.

8. When scallops are made on a single fabric thickness, trim excess fabric up to stitching line or use one of the edge finishes described on pages 119–121.

Chapter 9

SEWING MACHINE MAINTENANCE

BASIC MAINTENANCE

Over 80 percent of expensive service calls could be avoided by taking proper care of your sewing machine. Proper care involves three basic things: changing the needle often, keeping the machine clean, and keeping it well oiled.

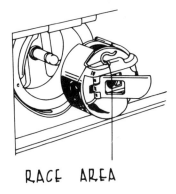

RACE AREA

Figure 9-1 The hook in the race area of a bobbin often wears out.

Changing Needles

1. Always use the correct type of needle for your machine.
2. Always use the appropriate-size needle for the thread and fabric you are using (see pages 31–34).
3. *Always change the needle after every garment.* Needles dull easily and will damage both your fabric and your machine. Many service problems are the result of rough, worn spots on the needle plate or on the hook in the race area near the bobbin (figure 9-1).
4. To insert needle correctly, consult sewing machine instruction book. A needle put in backward causes skipped stitches.
5. Avoid pulling too tightly on the fabric while sewing. This will bend the needle, which will subsequently damage the machine.

Cleaning

1. Use lint brush to clean around race area and under feed dog after each garment. Also dust away lint from tension controls. Check your machine instruction book for cleaning instructions.
2. Keep machine covered when not in use to prevent accumulation of dust and dirt particles.

Oiling

1. Remove needle and unplug the machine before oiling.
2. Use a pure sewing machine oil—one that has no detergents. Other oils will eventually cause the mechanisms to lock up.
3. Oil after every 8 to 12 hours of sewing time or once a month, whichever comes first.

To oil a flatbed sewing machine, tip the head back in the

cabinet or portable carrying case and move the flywheel back and forth by hand. Put a drop of oil at every moving part. Many free-arm machines have oiling points marked on the top cover and on the free arm; so it is unnecessary to remove cover plates for oiling. *Note:* Newer sewing machines have self-lubricating parts, and do not require oiling as frequently as older machines. However, to keep the machine running smoothly and vibration-free, be sure to oil the race area every 8 to 12 hours of sewing time. Check your machine instruction book for complete oiling information.

4. Oil the machine and let it run at full speed for about 2 minutes. Let it sit a few minutes, then wipe excess oil off the bed of the machine before sewing.

Skipped Stitches

Skipped stitches have become a problem in recent years, mostly due to the appearance of synthetic fabrics on the market. Skipped stitches normally can be traced to the needle, the thread, the presser foot, or the fabric.

The Needle

1. The needle is dull or bent. Change it after every garment.
2. The needle is placed incorrectly in the needle clamp. It is either backward or not all the way up in the needle clamp.
3. The wrong type of needle is being used for fabric.
4. The thread is too thick for the size needle being used.
5. With the needle in center position, the fabric does not have enough support from the presser foot and needle plate which can cause skipped stitches and puckered seams. The solution? Try using left needle position. This way, the needle is supported on three sides so the fabric will not move up and down with every stitch.

The Thread

1. The machine is threaded incorrectly.
2. Many brands of bargain thread are too stiff and coarse, making stitch formation difficult or impossible. Buy a good brand of thread.
3. The thread is the wrong type. Use all-cotton instead of cotton-wrapped polyester, or long-staple polyester.

The Presser Foot

1. The foot being used is not holding the fabric taut enough against the feed dog, so the fabric is being pulled up and down with every stitch. Use the foot which gives the most control possible for the specific sewing task (page 20).
2. There is not enough pressure on the presser bar to hold the fabric firmly. Increase pressure on the pressure control.

The Fabric

1. The fabric has a heavy finish on it which impairs stitch formation. Prewash the fabric before sewing (pages 29–30).
2. The machine skips stitches only on certain fabrics. Try all of the listed procedures before calling a repairman.

COMMON CAUSES OF SEWING MACHINE TROUBLE

Thread Breaking

1. Machine improperly threaded.
2. Thread is caught in slit of spool or under spool.
3. Thread is dry or of poor quality.
4. Tension is too tight.
5. Starting the machine with take-up lever in wrong position—always start and end sewing with take-up lever in highest position.
6. Needle is bent, blunt, or has a burr on it.
7. Needle is inserted incorrectly.
8. Thread too coarse for needle being used.
9. Needle plate has been nicked by the needle, so it is sharp and cuts the threads.

Needle Becomes Unthreaded

1. Take-up lever is not in correct position as you start sewing.
2. Thread ends not long enough. Allow thread tails of 3 to 4 inches at the start of sewing.

Needle Breaks

1. Excessive pulling on fabric while sewing bends the needle, and it may break if it hits the plate.
2. Needle is inserted incorrectly.
3. Needle is too fine for the type of fabric.

4. Bobbin was not wound evenly.

5. Thread is too thick for needle being used.

Uneven Stitches

1. Excessive pulling or holding fabric while sewing.

2. Unbalanced tension.

3. Thread is of poor quality or uneven thickness.

4. Needle hits pins—remove pins before sewing over them.

5. Pressue control is not in *full* position. Set control so there is maximum pressure between the foot and feed dog.

Fabric Puckers

1. Stitch is too *long* for the fabric.

2. Improper threading.

3. Thread is too heavy for fabric.

4. Needle is dull, making it difficult to pierce fabric.

5. Tensions are too tight.

6. The presser foot being *used* is not holding the fabric firmly against the feed dog.

7. If all else fails, try sewing over paper.

Threads Jam at Start of Sewing

1. Hold the threads to the *side* for the first few stitches.

2. Be sure the presser foot is down on thick fabrics.

Machine is Noisy

1. Clean and oil it.

2. If there is a punching sound, change the needle.

INDEX

141